SOUNDS GOOD 1
An Introduction to Music for the new Junior Cycle

Laura Lynch

The Educational Company of Ireland

First published 2018

The Educational Company of Ireland

Ballymount Road

Wakinstown

Dublin 12

www.edco.ie

A member of the Smurfit Kappa Group plc

978-1-84536-797-8

The paper used in this book comes from Managed Forests in Northern Europe For every tree felled, at least one new tree is planted

Editor: Peter Nickol

Proofreader: Kilmeny MacBride

Design: EMC Design

Layout: Compuscript

Cover: EMC

Cover Photography: Shutterstock

Illustrations: Global Blended Learning, Compuscript, Derry Dillon

Project editor: Lucy Taylor

The author would like to extend her thanks to all in Edco – particularly Emer Ryan, Declan Dempsey, Lucy Taylor and Peter Nickol, for their dedication and generous support and assistance in the completion of *Sounds Good 1: An introduction to Music for the new Junior Cycle*. I would like to thank my students, past and present, for their enthusiasm for music; you continue to be an inspiration and it has been my pleasure to be your teacher. I wish also to thank my parents for their sacrifice, support and infinite love. Deepest gratitude to Brien for his unconditional support and encouragement, and to Freddie and Pearl, the melody in my life.

Thanks to: Neil Moloney, Evan O'Sullivan and Kevin Donnelly for their contribution to the audio CD; Al Cowan in Sonic Studios; Eímear Noone; Zoë Conway; Donal Kearney; Steve Humphries; Copper and Zink; Gemma Ashcroft; Comhaltas.

Contents

Introduction v

   A Guide to *Sounds Good 1: An introduction to Music for the new Junior Cycle* vi

   Your *Sounds Good 1* CDs xiii

Acknowledgements xv

Unit 1 – My Music Passport 1

  1 Me and My Music 2

  2 My Life, My Soundtrack 5

  3 Mixtapes and Playlists 10

  4 Music in Our Lives 14

  5 Music and Community 19

Unit 2 – Elements of Music 24

  6 Pulse and Tempo 25

  7 Dynamics 29

  8 Pitch and Timbre 32

  9 Mood and Expression in Music 36

  10 Melody and Rhythm 39

Unit 3 – The Listening Lab 43

  11 Music and the Arts 44

  12 Active Listening 46

  13 Music History Timeline 48

  14 Texture 58

  15 Form 65

  16 Unit 3 Round-up 69

Unit 4 – The Conducting Lab 73

  17 Role of the Conductor 74

  18 How to Conduct 78

  19 The Orchestra 83

  20 Introduction to Notation 91

  21 Rhythms and Time Signatures 96

Chapters

Chapters

Chapters

Chapters

Unit 5 – Composing Lab 101

Chapters

22 Composing with Rhythm 102
23 Pitches and Notation 106
24 Composing with Melody 110
25 Composing with Form and Texture 114
26 Orchestral Scores 118
27 Experimental Music 120
28 Commercial Music 126

Unit 6 – Music of the World 129

Chapters

29 Oral Traditions 130
30 Irish Song Traditions 132
31 Irish Instrumental Traditions 138
32 The Preservation of Irish Music 146
33 Modern Developments in Irish Music 148

Unit 7 – Performing 151

Chapters

34 Performance for Wellbeing 152
35 Warming up the Voice 155
36 So Let's Sing 158
37 Body Music 163
38 The Performance Process 171

Unit 8 – Playing the Recorder 175

Chapters

39 Getting Started – First Notes 176
40 Progressing to C and D 179
41 Extending the Range: Low D and E 182
42 More Notes: Low C and F 186
43 Complex Notes: F sharp and High C sharp 189

Classroom Based Assessment 1 (CBA1) – The Composition Portfolio 196
Classroom Based Assessment 2 (CBA2) – Programme Note Guidelines 199
Glossary 201

Introduction

Welcome!

Welcome to *Sounds Good 1: An introduction to Music for the new Junior Cycle*, your textbook for Junior Cycle Music. As you begin your journey in your new school, you may be also beginning your experience of studying music as an academic subject. *Sounds Good 1: An introduction to Music for the new Junior Cycle* is an engaging and innovative textbook which places you at the centre of your learning and provides you with a suite of resources to guide you on this new adventure, whilst meeting the requirements of the Junior Cycle Music Specification. In all these new experiences I hope you will remember that music has been a part of your life for a long time. Music has been helping you to make sense of the world since you were a small baby. Music is a language that our hearts and minds recognise and respond to. In fact, music has been a good friend which has been with you always.

Sounds Good 1: An introduction to Music for the new Junior Cycle textbook will provide you with an opportunity to explore your relationship with music a little more and develop many important skills that will serve you well throughout your life. This textbook will support your learning as you engage with the Learning Outcomes set out in your subject specification. Throughout this book the concepts central to the teaching and learning of music are covered in the eight Units of Learning. New learning is revisited, directly and indirectly through the various units, whilst developing important skills and assessing your learning experience.

Development of Keys Skills, supporting your Wellbeing, and offering you opportunities for meaningful Assessment have been embedded in the Units of Learning set out in this textbook. Investigating, evaluating and reflecting on information whilst collaborating with your classmates will provide you with important opportunities to engage with each other, learn from each other and, most importantly, learn about yourself too.

It's important to take these opportunities to think, discover, research and explore as they will provide you with creative space to express your ideas and showcase the creative individual you are! Your *Sounds Good 1: An introduction to Music for the new Junior Cycle* textbook has been designed to seek out your individual talents of creativity, innovation and enterprise. This book will help you to build on your own musical knowledge and experience to date, whilst supporting you in progressing as you imagine, compose and perform music. You will be inspired by the creativity of other creative people you meet throughout this book.

I hope your *Sounds Good 1: An introduction to Music for the new Junior Cycle* will become your companion on your learning journey. Enjoy the adventure!

Laura Lynch

A Guide to *Sounds Good 1: An introduction to Music for the new Junior Cycle*

We hope you enjoy using *Sounds Good 1: An introduction to Music for the new Junior Cycle*.

The *Sounds Good 1* package includes:

Two CDs – a wide range of music that links to the book to help you to learn about and appreciate music

A whiteboard – for you to use at home and in class to practise writing down music

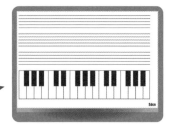

Keyboard Cover Flap – a visual aid to help you to identify notes and chords on the piano. It has been designed to help you engage with and explore new musical concepts covered in your textbook

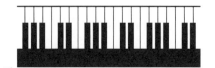

Self Assessment Post-its – at the end of each chapter for you to gather evidence of your learning, new key words and music you have listened to in each chapter

Music glossary – Musical terms you will encounter in this book, gathered and explained

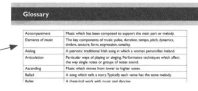

As you work through this book, there are important easy-to-follow symbols to help you. Below is an outline of what these symbols mean:

 Listen to a track on the CD

 Present in class

 Use your whiteboard

 Perform in class

 Investigate

 Listen

 Work together

 Report

Digital learning

Digital learning technologies enhance our learning experience. Using various technologies will help us to grow into creative and engaged thinkers. Technology promotes active learning and supports you in your development as a global citizen, participating fully in a global society.

Exploring the following digital software will support your learning.

Software	Apps	
◆ Audacity	◆ GarageBand	◆ Tone Pad
◆ Musescore	◆ Score Creator	◆ Acapella
◆ Finale	◆ Drum Genius	◆ iMovie
◆ Hooktheory	◆ Geometric Music	◆ Incredibox
◆ Reaper Digital Audio Workstation	◆ Just Press Record	◆ Music Memos

Key Skills

Learning about music will help to develop your **Key Skills.**

Key Skill	
Being Creative	Developing your imagination and creativity through group discussion, movement, visual thinking, peer teaching, creative use of technology and taking creative risks.
Communicating	Use communication skills to explore and express your emotions. Opportunities for performance or presentation: communicating with an audience, listening to and observing your classmates and developing an understanding of how to communicate your ideas help to develop this skill.
Working with Others	You will learn to negotiate relationships with your teacher and classmates during the many activities in your textbook; actively listening to each other, sharing ideas, rehearsing and performing together. A respectful music space, which values the contribution of each individual, will help you to collaborate effectively with others.
Staying Well	You will develop confidence as you contribute to decisions within group music – making activities and collaborative creative endeavours. You will develop resilience in the face of difficulties and a sense of satisfaction in the achievement of new goals.
Managing Myself	Developing personal goals and plans, reflecting and evaluating on your progress as you work through your textbook will give you a great sense of achievement. Try to identify and reflect on personal strengths and weaknesses; consider the choices you make and ask for help or feedback to help you to develop this skill further.
Being Literate	You can create music in response to different stimuli, such as images, texts, abstract ideas / moods / emotions or other melodic forms and fragments.
Being Numerate	You will work with numbers and make calculations to explore the relationships between different genres of music and you will identify similarities or differences in music through listening and composing tasks.
Managing Information and Thinking	Researching and working with information in various formats helps you to build these skills. You can explore digital devices to record your individual or group creations in order to share this content with each other and develop a portfolio of your work.

Music plays a significant role in staying well. Studying music will help you to feel confident, happy, healthy and connected to those around you. The units you will study in your new textbook are designed with your wellbeing in mind. As you work through this book you should evaluate how these topics have made a positive impact on your wellbeing. The wellbeing indicators you should consider include being:

Active: Sing, clap and dance whenever you can! Be confident and active in the physical activities in this book. Participating and keeping busy whilst you learn is fun and good for you!

Responsible: Take action to guard your wellbeing and the wellbeing of others. Make healthy choices and ensure you stay safe at all times.

Connected: Feeling you are connected to the people and places in your community is vital for feeling well. Be mindful that your actions and interactions impact on both your wellbeing and the wellbeing of others.

Resilient: Life is challenging! Being able to cope with the challenges that come your way can be difficult. Ensure that you know where you can seek help and believe firmly in what you can achieve in overcoming many of life's challenging moments.

Aware: Be aware of your thoughts, feelings and behaviours. Reflect on ways in which you learn; what helps you to learn?

Respected: You should feel listened to and valued always. In turn, try to show this to those you meet throughout your day. Building positive relationships with your teachers and classmates creates an environment of mutual respect that you will thrive within.

Learning Outcomes

'Learning outcomes are statements that describe what knowledge, understanding, skills and values students should be able to demonstrate having studied music in junior cycle. The learning outcomes set out in the following tables apply to all students. As set out here they represent outcomes for students at the end of their three years of study. The specification stresses that the learning outcomes are for three years and therefore the learning outcomes focused on at a point in time will not have been "completed" but will continue to support the students' learning in music up to the end of junior cycle.'

p.15 Specification for Junior Cycle Music

Learning Outcomes identify the knowledge and skills that you should acquire through your learning experiences, during the three years of junior cycle. As you explore *Sounds Good 1: An introduction to Music for the new Junior Cycle*, it's important to remember that the 36 Learning Outcomes have been unpacked to isolate intended learning for each Unit of this book, but are not completed, as recommended by the specification (see above). These important learning experiences are revisited directly and indirectly throughout this textbook, and in *Sounds Good 2*.

You will develop your knowledge and skills gradually as you engage and explore the content and learning experiences set out in your *Sounds Good* textbooks. The tables on pages x to xii contain the official 36 Learning Outcomes for Junior Cycle Music and identify where they are met in *Sounds Good 1: An introduction to Music for the new Junior Cycle*.

It is recommended that you take time to refer back to full Learning Outcomes when completing your Reflection and Evaluation sheets, found at the end of each unit. Reflecting on your learning experiences will involve evaluating new knowledge, understanding and skills gained as you progress through the Units of this book.

LO	Learning Outcome	UNIT
	Strand One: Procedural knowledge	
	Creating and exploring	
	Students should be able to:	
1.1	compose and perform or play back short musical phrases and support these phrases by creating rhythmic/melodic/harmonic ostinati to accompany them	2, 7
1.2	create and present a short piece, using instruments and/or other sounds in response to a stimulus.	4
1.3	design a harmonic or rhythmic accompaniment, record this accompaniment and improvise over this recording	5, 6
1.4	indicate chords that are suitable to provide harmonic support to a single melody line	8
	Participating and music-making	
	Students should be able to:	
1.5	read, interpret and play from symbolic representations of sounds	4, 7
1.6	listen to and transcribe rhythmic phrases of up to four bars and melodic phrases of up to two bars	5
1.7	perform music at sight through playing, singing or clapping melodic and rhythmic phrases	4, 7, 8
1.8	rehearse and perform pieces of music that use common structural devices and textures	7
1.9	demonstrate an understanding of a range of metres and pulses through the use of body percussion or other means of movement	2, 7
	Appraising and responding	
	Students should be able to:	
1.10	discuss the characteristics and defining features of contrasting styles of music represented in the local school or community	1
1.11	illustrate the structure of a piece of music through a physical or visual representation	3, 5
1.12	indicate where chord changes occur in extracts from a selection of songs	8
1.13	compare different interpretations or arrangements of a piece of Irish traditional or folk music, paying attention to musical elements and other influences	6
1.14	compare pieces of music that are similar in period and style by different composers from different countries	3

LO	Learning Outcome	UNIT
	Strand Two: Innovate and ideate	
	Creating and exploring	
	Students should be able to:	
2.1	experiment and improvise with making different types of sounds on a sound source and notate a brief piece that incorporates the sounds by devising symbolic representations for these sounds	2, 4, 8
2.2	create a musical statement (such as a rap or an advertising jingle) about a topical issue or current event and share with others the statement's purpose and development	5
2.3	adapt excerpts/motifs/themes from an existing piece of music by changing its feel, style, or underlying harmony	6
	Participating and music-making	
	Students should be able to:	
2.4	rehearse and present a song or brief instrumental piece; identify and discuss the performance skills and techniques that were necessary to interpret the music effectively	4, 6, 8
2.5	prepare and rehearse a musical work for an ensemble focusing on co-operation and listening for balance and intonation; refine the interpretation by considering elements such as clarity, fluency, musical effect and style	4, 7, 8
2.6	design a rhythmic or melodic ostinato and add layers of sound over the pattern as it repeats, varying the texture to create a mood piece to accompany a film clip or sequence of images	5, 8
2.7	create and present some musical ideas using instruments and/or found sounds to illustrate moods or feelings expressed in a poem, story or newspaper article	5
	Appraising and responding	
	Students should be able to:	
2.8	analyse the chordal structure of excerpts from a range of songs and compile a list of songs with similar chord structures and progressions	Sounds Good 2
2.9	distinguish between the sonorities, ranges and timbres of selections of instruments and voices; identify how these sounds are produced and propose their strengths and limitations in performance	4, 6
2.10	develop a set of criteria for evaluating a live or recorded performance; use these criteria to complete an in-depth review of a performance	8
2.11	evaluate the impact that technology is having on how we access music; propose ways that their music, and that of their fellow students, can be shared to reach a global audience	1, 6

LO	Learning Outcome	UNIT
	Strand Three: Culture and context	
	Creating and exploring	
	Students should be able to:	
3.1	collaborate with fellow students and peers to produce a playlist and a set of recordings to accompany a local historical event or community celebration	1, 6
3.2	examine and interpret the impact of music on the depiction of characters, their relationships and their emotions, as explored in instrumental music of different genres	3
3.3	make a study of a particular contemporary or historical musical style; analyse its structures and use of musical devices, and describe the influence of other styles on it	3, 4, 6
	ELEMENT: Participating and music-making	
	Students should be able to:	
3.4	compose and perform an original jingle or brief piece of music for use in a new advertisement for a product, and record the composition	5
3.5	devise and perform examples of incidental music that could be used in a variety of contexts or environments	8
	ELEMENT: Appraising and responding	
	Students should be able to:	
3.6	associate/match music excerpts to a variety of texts (words, film, language) and justify the reasons as to why this piece of music was chosen to match the text	3
3.7	compare compositions by two or more Irish composers or songwriters; use listening, background reading, and scores (where appropriate) to explain and describe differences and similarities in the compositions	3, 6
3.8	select a particular advertisement and analyse the role music plays in supporting the message and promoting the product	1, 2
3.9	investigate the influence of processing effects (e.g. distortion, reverb, compression) on the recording process; select some recordings and evaluate the use and effectiveness of such effects within them	8
3.10	discuss the principles of music property rights and explain how this can impact on the sharing and publishing of music	4, 6
3.11	explore the time allocated to Irish artists and performers on a variety of local or national Irish media and present these findings to their class	4, 6

Your *Sounds Good 1* CDs

CD 1		CD 2	
Track	**Page no.**	**Track**	**Page no.**
1 'Lullaby' by Brahms	5	1 'The Giraffe the Pelly and Me' by Roald Dahl	103
2 'Suantraí Suí' by Padraigín Ní Uallacháin with words by Rúairí Ó hUallacháin	5	2 Drum loop	104
3 Prelude in E minor, Opus 28 No. 4 by Chopin	26	3–4 Identifying rhythms	104
4 'Flight of the Bumble Bee' by Rimsky-Korsakov	26	5–8 Rhythm dictation exercises	105
5 Extract from 'The Firebird' by Stravinsky	29	9 'Mars' from *The Planets* by Holst	116
6 Overture to 'The Bartered Bride' by Smetana	30	10 'Trepak' (Russian dance) from 'The Nutcracker Suite' by Tchaikovsky	118
7 'Lullaby' by Brahms	30	11 *Solitude* by Hans-Christophe Steiner	120
8 'Worthy is the Lamb' from *Messiah* by Handel	31	12 'Sonata No. 6' from *Sonatas and Interludes* by John Cage	124
9 'The Grand Old Duke of York'	31	13 'Siúil a Rún' performed by Acabella	132
10–19 10 sounds to identify	33	14 'Ordinary Man' performed by Christy Moore	133
20 'The Swan' from *Carnival of the Animals* by Saint-Saens	38	15 'The Parting Glass' performed by The High Kings	135
21 'The Liberty Bell' by Sousa	38	16 'The Parting Glass' performed by Cara Dillon	135
22 'La Mer' by Debussy	45	17 'Na Páipéir á Saighneáil' performed by Eimear Arkins	136
23 'The Confrontation' from *Les Misérables* by Schönberg	47	18 'Táimse im' Chodhladh' performed by Dolores Keane	137
24 'Galliard Ballaglia' by Samuel Scheidt	49	19 'Táimse im' Chodhladh' performed by Zoë Conway	137
25 'Pantomime' from *Les Petits Riens* by Mozart	51	20 'Aisling Gheal' played by Mary Bergin	138
26 'The Blue Bird and Princess Florine' from *The Sleeping Beauty* by Tchaikovsky	54	21 'Cooley's Reel' played by Neil Moloney and Evan O'Sullivan	143
27 Gregorian chant – 'Conditor alme siderum'	59	22 'Off to California'	144
28 'The Confrontation' from *Les Misérables* by Schönberg	61	23 'The Banshee'	144
29 'Duel of the Fates' from *Star Wars: The Phantom Menace*	61	24 'Out On the Ocean'	144
30 'His Yoke Is Easy' from *Messiah* by Handel	61	25 'Planxty Irwin' played by Patrick Ball	145
31 'The Viennese Musical Clock' from the *Háry János Suite* by Kodály	65	26 'Buaile Mo chroí' performed by Karan Casey	148
32 'Golliwogg's Cakewalk' from *Children's Corner* by Debussy	69	27 'Somewhere along the road' performed by Steeleye Span	158
33 Piano Concerto No. 2 in C minor by Rachmaninov	69	28 'Thula Klizeo' performed by Elementary Honor Choir	166
34 'Can-Can' from *Orpheus in the Underworld* by Offenbach	81	29 Piano accompaniment to 'Thula Klizeo'	166
35 'The Grand Old Duke of York'	81	30–33 Sing back melodies	170
36 'Morning has Broken'	81	34 Piano accompaniment to 'Little John'	180
37 Minuet in G from the *Notebook for Anna Magdalena* by Bach	81	35 Piano accompaniment to 'Red River Valley'	185
38 4th movement (Allegro) from String Quartet in C minor, Op.18 No. 4 by Beethoven	81	36 Piano accompaniment to 'Oh Sinner Man'	188
39 The 'Hallelujah Chorus' from *Messiah* by Handel	81	37 Piano accompaniment to 'Bobby Shafto'	190
40 'Theme' from *The Young Person's Guide to the Orchestra* by Britten	84	38 Piano accompaniment to 'Lullaby' by Brahms	193
41 'Woodwind' from *The Young Person's Guide to the Orchestra* by Britten	85		
42 'Strings' from *The Young Person's Guide to the Orchestra* by Britten	86		
43 'Brass' from *The Young Person's Guide to the Orchestra* by Britten	87		
44 'Percussion' from *The Young Person's Guide to the Orchestra* by Britten	88		
45 'Fugue' from *The Young Person's Guide to the Orchestra* by Britten	89		

Acknowledgements

All music in this book has been reproduced with the kind permission of the publishers, agents, composers or their estates as follows:

'Lullaby' by Brahms permission Naxos; 'Suantrai Suí' traditional by Padraigín Ní Uallacháin with words by Rúairí Ó hUallacháin permission Pádraigín Ní Uallacháin MCPS/IMRO available on www. irishsong.com; Prelude in E minor, Opus 28 No. 4 by Chopin permission Naxos; 'Flight of the Bumble Bee' by Rimsky-Korsakov permission Naxos; extract from 'The Firebird' by Stravinsky permission Naxos/Profil; overture to 'The Bartered Bride' by Smetana permission Naxos; 'Lullaby' by Brahms permission Naxos; 'Worthy is the Lamb' from *Messiah* by Handel permission Naxos/Signum; 'The Grand Old Duke of York' recorded by Kevin Donnelly; 10–19 10 sounds to identify – from Getty Images and recorded by Kevin Donnelly; 'The Swan' from *Carnival of the Animals* by Saint-Saens permission NaxosOndine; 'The Liberty Bell' by Sousa permission Naxos/Altissimo; 'La Mer' by Debussy permission Naxos; 'The Confrontation' from *Les Misérables* by Schönberg permission First Night Music and Alan Boublil Music; 'Galliard Ballaglia' by Samuel Scheidt/Allegretto; 'Pantomime' from *Les Petits Riens* by Mozart permission Naxos/Hungaraton; 'The Blue Bird and Princess Florine' from *The Sleeping Beauty* by Tchaikovsky permission Naxos; Gregorian chant – 'Conditor alme siderum' permission Naxos/Griffin Records; 'The Confrontation' from *Les Misérables* by Schönberg permission First Night Music and Alan Boublil Music; 'Duel of the Fates' from *Star Wars* © Silva Screen Records Ltd; 'His Yoke Is Easy' from *Messiah* by Handel permission Naxos/Swedish Society; 'The Viennese Musical Clock' from the *Háry János Suite* by Kodály – permission Naxos/Nimbus; 'Golliwogg's Cakewalk' from *Children's Corner* by Debussy permission Naxos; Piano Concerto No. 2 in C minor by Rachmaninov permission Naxos; 'Can-Can' from *Orpheus in Underworld* by Offenbach permission Naxos; 'Morning has Broken' permission Naxos/Musical Concepts; Minuet in G from the *Notebook for Anna Magdalena* by Bach permission Naxos/Brilliant Classics; 4th movement (Allegro) from String Quartet in C minor, Op.18 No. 4 by Beethoven permission Naxos/Hungaraton; The 'Hallelujah Chorus' from *Messiah* by Handel permission Naxos/Signum; 'Theme' from *The Young Person's Guide to the Orchestra* by Britten permission Naxos; 'Woodwind' from *The Young Person's Guide to the Orchestra* by Britten permission Naxos; 'Strings' from *The Young Person's Guide to the Orchestra* by Britten permission Naxos; 'Brass' from *The Young Person's Guide to the Orchestra* by Britten permission Naxos; 'Percussion' from *The Young Person's Guide to the Orchestra* by Britten permission Naxos; 'Fugue' from *The Young Person's Guide to the Orchestra* by Britten permission Naxos. 'The Giraffe the Pelly and Me' by Roald Dahl, © The Roald Dahl Story Company Limited, recorded in the studio by Evan O'Sullivan; 'Mars' from *The Planets* by Holst permission Naxos; 'Trepak' (Russian dance) from *The Nutcracker Suite* by Tchaikovsky permission Naxos/Gramola; *Solitude* graphic score and recording by permission of Hans-Christophe Steiner; *Towards an Unbearable Lightness* graphic score by Carl Bergstrøm-Nielsen with permission of CoMA; 'Sonata No. 6' from *Sonatas and Interludes* by John Cage permission Naxos; 'Siúil a Rún' performed by Acabella permission Yvonne Crotty; 'Ordinary Man' performed by Christy Moore permission Peter Hames and Christy Moore with assistance from Paddy Doherty (Crossroads Music); 'The Parting Glass' performed by The High Kings permission Celtic Collections; 'The Parting Glass' performed by Cara Dillon permission Charcoal Records; 'Na Páipéir á Saighneáil' performed by Eimear Arkins permission Comhaltas Cealtoiri Eireann, 32 Belgrave Square, Monkstown, Co. Dublin; 'Táimse im' Chodhladh' performed by Dolores Keane permission Dolphin Music Group; 'Táimse im' Chodhladh' performed by Zoë Conway permission Tara Music Group; 'Aisling Gheal' played by Mary Bergin permission Gael Linn/MCPSI; 'Cooley's Reel' played by Neil Moloney and Evan O'Sullivan; 'Off to California' permission Naxos/The Gift of Music; 'The Banshee' permission Naxos/The Gift of Music; 'Out in the Ocean' permission Naxos/The Gift of Music; 'Planxty Irwin' played by Patrick Ball permission Naxos/Fortuna Records; 'Buaile Mo chroi' performed by Karan Casey permission Whirlie Records; 'Somewhere along the road' performed by Steeleye Span permission Park Records; 'Thula Klizeo' performed by Elementary Honor Choir permission Soundwave Recordings; piano accompaniments performed by Kevin Donnelly.

The authors and publisher wish to thank the following for permission to reproduce photos and other material. GagliardiImages/Shutterstock, p1, LStockStudio/Shutterstock p1, Solei/Shutterstock p1, Billion Photos/Shutterstock p2, coldaf-79/Shutterstock.com p2, Anthony Correia/Shutterstock. com p3, Drbouz/Getty p3, Tetiana Saienko/Shutterstock p5, Global Blended Learning p6, Peter Nickol p8, MPIX/Shutterstock p10, Antonio Guillem/Shutterstock p11, paul abbitt rml/Alamy p11, Kachalkina Veronika/Shutterstock p14, Martin Good/Shutterstock p14, 1000 Words/Shutterstock p14, Fotografiecor.nl/Shutterstock p14, Christian Bertrand/Shutterstock.com p14, Stephen Barnes/

My Music Passport

In this unit

From the moment we are born we are in a musical world. This unit will provide you with an opportunity to reflect on your own personal musical ideas and experiences. We will evaluate how these are reflected in your everyday life and in your community. You will have an opportunity to explore different genres and collaborate with your new classmates to research, reflect on and evaluate the role music plays in our lives.

Intended learning

Discuss the characteristics of contrasting styles of music represented in your local school or community.

1.10
2.11, 3.1
3.8

Evaluate the impact that technology is having in how we access music; propose ways that music can be shared.

Collaborate with fellow students to produce a playlist and a set of recordings for a community celebration.

Select a particular advertisement and analyse the role music plays in supporting the message and promoting the product.

Your fingerprint is an outward marker of your individuality.

Each one of us is a unique individual, with our own history from the moment we are born. Think of all the ways in which we are unique. Look around the class and discuss this. There may be some common characteristics, but individually we should celebrate and embrace our unique identity.

This unit starts with your unique relationship with music and explores the way music reaches into all our lives.

Me and My Music

Music is different for all of us, and we have experienced it in many different ways since we were born. Filling in this form will help us to identify our unique musical preferences and interests.

1 Name _____

2 Date of birth _____

3 National anthem _____

4 I listen to music:

every day ☐

sometimes ☐

often ☐

never ☐

5 The last piece of music I listened to was

_____

6 I listen to music most when I feel:

happy ☐   calm ☐

sad ☐   energetic ☐

tired ☐

7 My favourite type of music is _____

8 I am a member of:

a music school ☐   an orchestra ☐

a band ☐   a musical society ☐

a choir ☐

9 I listen to music on:

radio ☐   phone ☐

iPod ☐   other ☐

10 My favourite band or singer is _____

The genre of music they perform is _____

11 My favourite song is _____

12 Do you have a favourite song lyric? Tell us about it, and why you like it

_____

_____

13 I love to sing when _____

14 I can play an instrument: yes ☐ no ☐ What instrument? _____

15 If I could learn to play an instrument I would choose _____

16 My favourite instrument to listen to is _____

Because _____

17 My favourite radio station is _____

18 I download music using _____

19 I prefer: listening to music ☐ playing music ☐

Because _____

20 Others have inspired my musical tastes: yes ☐ no ☐

One example is _____

Genres

'Genre' is the word we use for a type of music, for instance, country, folk, pop, jazz, classical, brass band, etc. It's a bit like 'style', except that you can have different styles of music even within one genre.

No one has to restrict their taste to one genre. It's good to have a varied taste in music.

Share-and-compare class survey

 In pairs, introduce yourself. Share your answers with your classmate and complete the share-and-compare box below.

My name:		My partner's name:	
	Self		**Partner**
Favourite **genre**			
Favourite band			
Guitar or piano?			
iPod playlist or radio?			
Experienced live music?			
Plays an instrument?			
Favourite instrument			
Likes to sing?			
Favourite film theme tune			

My partner's name:	
Similarities we found	Differences we found
What I've learned about my classmate	
What song would you like to listen to after completing this activity? Why?	What song would you recommend your classmate listen to, and why?

What stuck with you?

Evaluate your learning in this chapter. List what stuck with you and new key words.

Music for my wellbeing

Think about how music sometimes helps how you feel. What music do you like to choose for these purposes?

Music for calmness

1 _____

2 _____

Music for exercise

1 _____

2 _____

Music that makes me happy

1 _____

2 _____

Music that reduces stress or worry

1 _____

2 _____

Lullabies

The oldest children's songs are lullabies – songs to help a baby fall asleep. Lullabies can be found in every human culture. Nowadays babies often fall asleep to the sound of a music box in their nursery, but traditionally women sang or hushed babies to sleep using lullabies.

Did you include a **lullaby** in your questionnaire? Maybe you can remember one from your own childhood.

 Listen to this lullaby. The tune is by Brahms. Can you describe the music? This melody has been put onto many mechanical music boxes; can you say why this might be?

An Irish lullaby is called a '**suantraí**'. Ireland's song tradition is full of beautiful suantraí, which were sung for centuries in homes throughout the country at bedtime.

 Listen to 'Suantraí Sí', which means 'A fairy lullaby'. 'Suantraí Sí' was put to music by Padraigín Ní Uallacháin, with words written by her brother Rúairi Ó hUallacháin. As you listen, follow the words.

Suantraí sí, a linbhín	*Fairy lullaby, my little child*
Luasc go mall sa chliabhán	*Swing slowly in the cradle*
Lú lá luí, a linbhín	*Lu la lee, my little child*
Dún do shúil, a naíonán	*Close your eyes, little infant*
Seoithín seoithín seoithín seó	*Lulla lulla lullaby*
Seoithín seoithín seoithín seó	*Lulla lulla lullaby*
Seoithín seoithín seoithín seó	*Lulla lulla lullaby*
Suantraí sí, a linbhín,	*Fairy lullaby, my little child*
A thaiscidh, a stór	*My darling, my love*
Luí go socair, luí go ciúin	*Lie quietly, lie calmly*
Codladh sámh, a ghrághil	*Sleep well, little fair one*
Fan id' shuan, a thaiscidh buan	*Stay asleep forever, my love*
Go n-éirí tú ar maidin	*Til you wake in the morning*

1 Describe the introduction to the song _____

2 Do you hear a male or female vocalist? _____

3 Choose one line you feel is particularly calm and restful

_____

4 **Repetition** is common in lullabies – why do you think this might be?

_____

5 Did you like this song? _____

6 How did it make you feel? _____

7 Can you identify **features** of the singer's performance?

_____

8 Can you name another Irish song? _____

9 If you were composing a melody for a **lullaby**, what instruments would you choose to play it? Give reasons for your answer.

_____

_____

10 Do you listen to music to help you sleep? If so, what **genre** of music do you choose?

_____

Nursery rhymes

A nursery rhyme is a traditional poem or song for children, sometimes with an educational purpose. When we are young, music is often used as a clever way of teaching new knowledge and skills. Nursery rhymes are full of **repetition**: repeated language and rhythms, paired together, make an effective way of learning.

Here is a good example:

> Head, shoulders, knees and toes, knees and toes
> Head, shoulders, knees and toes, knees and toes
> And eyes and ears and mouth and nose
> Head, shoulders, knees and toes, knees and toes

 'Head, shoulders, knees and toes' has repeated rhythm patterns. Try clapping the words instead of singing them in order to hear the rhythms more clearly. Count four beats in, so you start together. Then be careful to stay in time with each other. Teamwork!

Evaluate and describe the educational value of another nursery rhyme you learned at school.

6

My unique soundtrack

In our questionnaire on page 2 we took time to appreciate what makes us unique. We shared our musical experiences which have taken us to where we are today. We recognised the effect music can have on us and our feelings.

Music connects straight to our mind and emotions. Music can motivate us, calm us, inspire us – and sometimes upset, annoy or distract us.

Music can be a wonderful companion in life. A song can bring to mind vibrant memories of people, places and experiences from our past. Or it can evoke emotions connected to the experiences we have had. Hearing music from our past has a powerful effect on memory, like looking at an old photo; it can cause precious memories to come flooding back to us in an instant.

Let's create a soundtrack that best represents you and your unique life.

Think about your life until now and recognise:

◆ Major events that have inspired you, shaped you or influenced you.

◆ Moments in your life that are particularly memorable.

◆ Moments that may have influenced how you see the world.

Create a list of important experiences or people in your life.

1
2
3
4
5

Compile a list of songs or pieces of music that remind you of these times in your life. What do you like – or even dislike – about each one?

1
2
3
4
5

Like a **music producer**, try to consider the sequence for your chosen songs. Ideally, they should be listed in the **chronological order** of the events they document. This way, the music tells the story of your life; it will be meaningful for you to listen to.

In the grid below, list the track order with the artist or group who are performing the song. Also name the experience this song has been chosen to represent.

A **music producer** oversees the creation of recordings and albums. It can be a creative and influential role.

Track no.	Song title	Artist/Composer
1		
	Experience	
2		
3		
4		
5		

Chronological order means arranging things in time order.

Making a CD of your soundtrack

To make a CD of your soundtrack, what else does it need?

◆ A **title**. All albums are given a title. Sometimes it is a song from the album and sometimes not. Choose a name for your album.

Album name _____

Reason for giving this title

_____

◆ The other thing your album needs is a **cover**. Albums have a cover that has been created to make the album visually unique and distinct from other albums. Images created for album covers are usually representative of the album title or the theme of the material included on the CD. Sometimes it's a photograph of the performers, or an artist may create a piece of artwork instead. The cover may be the front of a booklet with information about the tracks or with the lyrics.

Design your CD cover. What name and what image will best represent you? List the song titles you have chosen on the back.

A blank template for a CD cover can be found in the teacher's book that accompanies this book.

Instead of including the lyrics in the CD case, you could compose a reflective letter to the listener. For each song, reflect on the experiences, people, places and events that inspired you to choose it.

You can use guide below to help you begin writing.

<u>Address the letter</u>

Dear Listener

<u>Introduce yourself</u>

Who are you?

<u>Purpose in creating this soundtrack</u>

What is this album you have created, and why?

<u>The songs on the soundtrack</u>

Indicate each song's importance to you. How does it make you feel?

Did you enjoy creating your soundtrack? Give a reason for your answer.

_____

What advice would you give to others?

_____

 Give a short presentation of your work to the class. Identify which part of your soundtrack you would like to share with your classmates. Play the song and explain why it was chosen.

What stuck with you?

Evaluate your learning in this chapter. List what stuck with you and new key words.

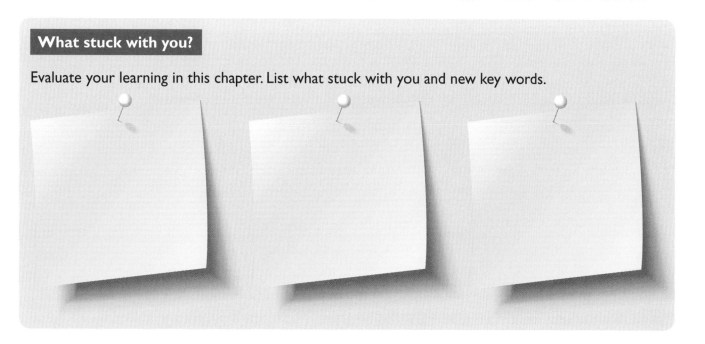

Mixtapes and playlists: these terms mean the same thing – your personal choice of tracks, brought together in one place. Mixtapes got their name from the cassette tapes that were the popular way of storing recorded music in the 1970s and 80s. In more recent years, iPods and then smartphones became the way to record and store music, but many people still like to use the word 'mixtapes'.

Cassette tapes encouraged us to compile our favourite songs in one place

My top 5

 What are your five favourite songs or pieces of music just now? List your current playlist below.

	Title	Artist
1		
2		
3		
4		
5		

Think about when you are likely to use your playlist. What do your five songs have that appeals to you? Maybe you haven't given this much thought before. Complete the form on page 13, taking some time to consider why the songs you have listed have a particular effect on you. Think about:

◆ Instruments

◆ Themes/topics

◆ Genre

◆ The lyrics

◆ The singer's style

◆ The story told in the song

Write down what appealed to you when choosing each song, using the form on the next page.

1 Title _____
2 Title _____
3 Title _____
4 Title _____
5 Title _____

Questionnaire

1 Compare similarities between the songs or pieces you have chosen.

_____

2 How many different **genres** are heard during this playlist? _____

3 What do you think your playlist tells us about you? _____

_____

_____

4 When would you listen to this particular playlist and why? _____

_____

Creating playlists for different situations

The **playlists** we create will change frequently, or we may have several different playlists to choose from. Sometimes we may decide to create a playlist to suit an event or an activity. Below are two scenarios requiring a playlist. Working singly or in pairs, choose one, and decide which songs you would include.

Scenario 1

You are going on a long car journey this weekend with your family. You decide to take earphones with you: listening to music is a great way to relax and enjoy the scenery along the way. What music would you like to hear?

Scenario 2

Your school rugby team has reached the final of the schools cup. What playlist would be suitable to be played before the game begins? Think of music which would create the desired atmosphere.

 With your partner (if you are working in pairs), choose your scenario, then decide on your playlist and list your choices below.

Scenario			
	Title	**Artist/Composer**	**Genre**
1			
2			
3			
4			
5			

Questionnaire

1 Which scenario did you choose, and why?

_____

2 What problems did you face compiling this playlist?

_____

3 Did you pick any instrumental music? _____

4 Identify the type of music that suits a car journey.

_____

5 Identify the type of music heard at sporting events.

_____

6 Argue the role of music at events such as these.

_____

7 Comment on how the music you have chosen may appeal to the listener.

_____

Discuss together other situations when a playlist could be useful. Do you find music helpful when studying? Or exercising? Or when you are preparing to sleep? Can you add three more possibilities to the list?

1 _____

2 _____

3 _____

Your home playlist

If possible, make a **playlist** at home. Use it, but don't be afraid to revisit it and make changes to it. You may find you've chosen a song that's too distracting to study with or that makes it difficult to relax. Taking time to put together music that makes an activity more enjoyable is always worth doing!

Chosen activity for this playlist	
Song title	Reason for choosing this song
1	
2	
3	
4	
5	

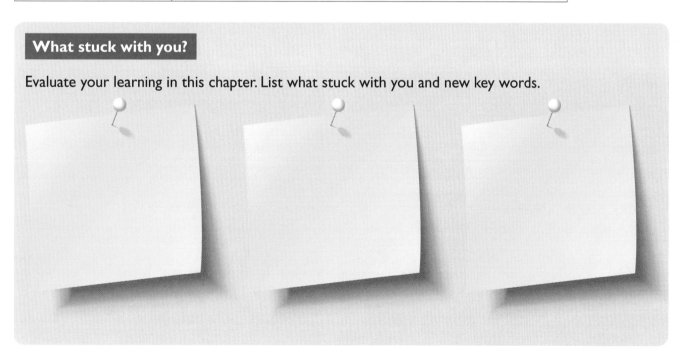

What stuck with you?

Evaluate your learning in this chapter. List what stuck with you and new key words.

Live music

When we talk about 'live music', what do we mean? When is music 'live' and when isn't it?

◆ What was the last piece of live music you enjoyed?

_____

◆ How often do you listen to live music?

_____

◆ Why are live performances so enjoyable?

_____

> Since the beginning of time, music has been about human beings communicating with each other. The word 'communicate' comes from the Latin *communicare*, which means 'to share'. Live music has existed since prehistoric times and has always been an important part of community life. Discuss the various kinds of live music shown in these photos.

Performers interacting with an audience is a very special experience, which is exciting for those listening.

Live performances may be by a single musician or by an **ensemble** such as an orchestra, choir or band. Concerts are held in a wide variety of settings, from private houses and small theatres through to large concert halls, entertainment venues and even sports stadiums. Can you recognise either of these Irish venues?

What live performances have you experienced? Choose one experience and discuss:

1 Who was performing? _____

2 Where was the performance? _____

3 Identify the genre the music belongs to. _____

4 List which instruments were used. _____

5 Was it an enjoyable experience for you? _____

6 Describe how the music made you feel? _____

_____

7 If you won tickets to a live performance, who would you like to see perform live?

_____

Concert promotion

Performances can be advertised in various ways: in newspapers and magazines, on community notice boards, on social media and email lists.

 Posters are particularly important. Look at these posters and discuss what makes a good poster. What information does a promoter need to include? _____

_____

_____

Where else could concerts be promoted? _____

Film Music

Film music is used in a film to accompany action and to **illustrate** emotion or mood, creating an atmosphere.

◆ What was the last movie you watched?

_____

◆ What was it about? _____

◆ Who were the main characters in it?

_____

◆ Can you remember the music in it? _____

◆ What's your all-time favourite movie and why? _____

◆ Name your favourite piece of film music? _____

◆ Can you name the **composer**? _____

◆ Why do you think this piece of music was chosen for the movie?

_____

◆ Do you think the music illustrated the story line from the movie?

_____

◆ How do you think the composer did this?

_____

Silent movies

The earliest films – black and white movies from the 1890s to the 1920s – had no soundtrack and were often accompanied by a live pianist or organist playing in the cinema.

Choose a piece of film music. Listen to it, and critique it below.

Name of film	
Name of director	
Name of composer	
What I thought of the music	
What I thought the composer was trying to **illustrate**: what emotion, mood or atmosphere is suggested.	

Film Scores

Music which has been created for a film is called a **film score**. It is original music, specially written. Some composers specialise in writing film scores. The music is designed to create an atmosphere or evoke an emotion to match a particular scene. The film's director offers guidance to the composer. Film scores include a wide range of genres and are created to accompany the action or story as it unfolds, throughout the entire movie.

Most film composers begin to compose when filming has been completed but the film is still being edited; this allows the music to slot into the film. Sometimes the composer starts work before filming begins, using the script as inspiration.

The composer **orchestrates** his or her music for the musicians who will play it, taking account of the different instruments. Once this process is complete, the **sheet music** is printed, a separate **part** for each player, ready for performance. Groups of musicians who perform together are called **ensembles**. Ensembles employed to perform film scores are sometimes large orchestras such as the London Symphony Orchestra.

Typically, the orchestra performs in front of a large screen depicting the film, so the conductor can watch the action. Both the **conductor** and musicians wear headphones to hear important sounds and instructions. This helps to synchronise the music with the film.

Born in 1932, John Williams is one of the most successful of all film composers. He wrote scores for the *Star Wars* series, *Jaws* and the *Harry Potter* series

Some films have a completely different kind of **soundtrack**: not specially written music at all but a compilation of pre-existing music, usually well-known pop songs, chosen because the director considered that they would match the character of the film.

Soundtrack	Film score
Compilation of songs used in a film but not specifically composed for the film	Original music, composed specifically for the film

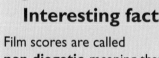

Interesting fact

Film scores are called **non-diegetic**, meaning that the music is played over the film and cannot be heard by the characters on screen. Music which comes from within the story and can be heard by characters in the film – for instance if a band is playing as part of the scene – is called **diegetic** music.

Reflect on your learning:

1 What is a film score? _____

2 Who creates a film score? _____

3 Outline why a film score is important. _____

4 Explain the term **'illustrative music'**. _____

5 Propose some questions you would need to ask before you begin creating a film score?

_____

_____

Research activity

 Research a film released in Irish cinemas recently.

Write a review of the film score for *Hot Press* magazine. Include relevant information about the film itself – genre, director, plot – and evaluate how the film score reflects this. Include information about the composer.

Music in Advertising

Music plays a big part in advertising. List some examples you can think of.

_____   _____   _____

Many TV or radio ads use a short burst of music called a **jingle**. The most effective jingles are the ones you can easily recall or that get stuck in your head. An effective jingle can ensure success for a product.

In recent years, advertising has also made use of pop songs. Popular hits can help boost a product by association: we make the connection, or the advertiser hopes we will.

Choose one advertising campaign with a prominent jingle, and analyse how the music helps the campaign.

Film composer Hans Zimmer working on *Spirit: Stallion of the Cimarron* (2002). Even if the music is eventually played by a large orchestra, much of a film composer's work is done in his or her studio, surrounded by keyboards and computer screens. Hans Zimmer's scores include *The Lion King* and the *Pirates of the Caribbean* series

Name of product _____

Type or style of music (your description) _____

List instruments or voices used _____

What type of mood do you think the jingle encourages us to feel?

_____

 Working in groups, choose an advertisement which uses music to support the message or product they wish to promote. Evaluate the role the music plays in this advert.

Present your findings to your class.

Music jingles on TV and radio can affect our buying decisions

What stuck with you?

Evaluate your learning in this chapter. List what stuck with you and new key words.

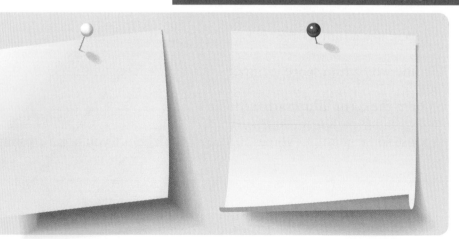

What does 'community' mean? Brainstorm, and use the diagram below to group all the words and ideas that come to mind when you think of community.

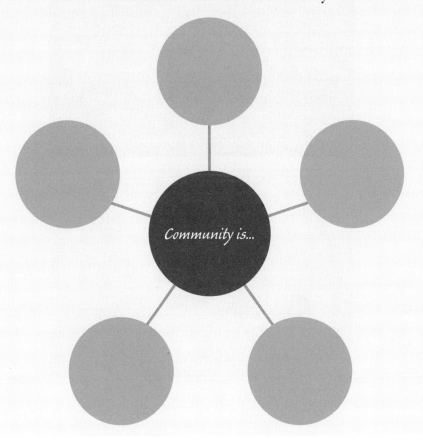

Community is...

Community can be experienced in many different ways. It can mean a geographical place: a town, suburb or local area. Community is also about relationships and about people coming together.

Community requires relationships between people. Earlier in this chapter we celebrated our uniqueness, but relationships with others are just as important. To feel part of our community we must be open to working with others.

In this chapter we will look at the role of music in our own community. Music is shared and enjoyed every day within our community – as it is in communities throughout the world.

Humans have a universal need to make and share music. It encourages wellness and gives musicians a sense of connection with their audience. Involvement in community music raises people's spirits. Even just going to watch a local group perform is an enjoyable experience and can make you feel part of that community.

Name two music groups in your local community.

1
2

What types of community music groups are there?

- Community choirs
- Youth orchestras
- Children's choirs
- Marching bands
- Accordion bands
- Céilí bands
- School choirs
- Ukelele bands
- Folk groups
- Church choirs
- Music schools
- Musical societies

 Discuss:

- Looking at the list above and at the photos, what do these groups have in common?
  Do they represent separate communities, or are they part of a larger community? Or a bit of both?

- What different types of community are there? Are there other communities in your locality with their own music? Could you do anything to connect with them?

- Are you a member of a community music group in your school?

 Identify one type of community music group and research the music they perform and listen to. Present your findings to the class.

Comhaltas Ceoltóirí Éireann  COMHALTAS

Comhaltas Ceoltóirí Éireann is the biggest community music organisation in Ireland. It was set up in 1951 in Mullingar. It promotes Irish music, song, dance and language.

Over the years, its work has spread to other countries. There are more than 420 branches worldwide! Do you know your closest CCÉ branch?

Comhaltas Ceoltóirí Éireann translates as 'Gathering of Musicians of Ireland'. It brings people together to enjoy Irish music. Songs and music are passed from one generation to another.

Comhaltas volunteers run weekly classes where young people learn to play traditional music. They also learn about song, dance and language. There are about 1,200 CCÉ music classes per week.

CCÉ also runs:

◆ **Fleadhanna Ceoil:** Over 25,000 young people compete at 44 Fleadhanna Ceoil each year. Seven of these take place in Britain and North America. **Fleadh Cheoil na hÉireann** was held in Ennis, Co. Clare in 2017 and 450,000 people attended the nine-day festival.

◆ **Summer Schools/Workshops:** These include 'Scoil Éigse', which is a week-long course.

◆ **Comhaltas National Folk Orchestra of Ireland**

◆ **Scrúdu Ceol Tíre:** This is a graded exam in performance, aural awareness, musical literacy and discussion/history of the music. Have you done an SCT exam?

◆ **TTCT:** This is a teaching diploma course.

◆ **Music archives/resources:** Comhaltas produces CDs, DVDs and books. It also runs a *Trad is Fab* programme for Primary Schools. You will find a weekly online audiovisual recording COMHALTASLIVE on its website, www. comhaltas.ie. Comhaltas Traditional Music Archive is also available online.

Comhaltas branches work with other community and voluntary groups. They organise and perform at local, national and international events.

Making a collective effort for greater good in the community is very important to Comhaltas Ceoltóirí Éireann. Maybe this year you will organise a TRAD FOR TRÓCAIRE seisiúin in your school community. You will find information on the Trócaire website (www.trocaire.org).

 Research and discuss the role of one other music organisation in your local community.

Reflections on music in the community

1   What gives people a sense of belonging in a community?

_____

_____

2   How important are factors such as cooperation, sharing and communication for the success of a community?

_____

_____

3   Comment on how music can fulfil a community's needs.

_____

_____

4   Indicate what we can do to support the work of community music groups.

_____

_____

What stuck with you?

Evaluate your learning in this chapter. List what stuck with you and new key words.

Reflection and Evaluation Sheet

Unit title:

Music I listened to:

Learning and exploring

I really enjoyed…

Something interesting I learned…

I excelled at…

My biggest challenge was…

I overcame this by…

I would like to learn more about…

New key words

Skills I developed in this unit…

This unit reminded me of learning about…

Goal setting…

-
-
-

Rate your learning

Elements of Music

In this unit

In this unit you will develop your music vocabulary and explore expressive elements in a piece of music. Through exploring, understanding and appreciating the expressive elements found in musical works you will acquire the skills necessary for analysing music. In choosing and listening to the music of others you will develop your ability to interpret the expressive qualities found in music and a composer's intentions during the creative process. You will collaborate with others to creatively demonstrate your understanding of musical elements through imagining and creating sounds and composing short musical motifs.

Intended learning

Compose and perform or play back short musical phrases and experiment with rhythm by creating rhythmic ostinati.

1.1

2.1, 2.9

3.2, 3.8

Experiment and improvise with making different types of sounds on a sound source.

Distinguish between the timbres of selections of instruments and voices; identify how these sounds are produced.

Select a particular advertisement and analyse the role music plays in supporting the message and promoting the product.

In the first unit of this book we looked at our individual music preferences and the important benefits of music in our lives. Listening to music comes easily to us, but learning to talk about music in detail, using musical terminology, may not be so easy.

In this unit we will study the fundamentals of music and gather the terminology we need to accurately describe the music we are listening to. By the end of the unit, you will have a new vocabulary of music, which will enable you to describe in detail the components of music and how they work together.

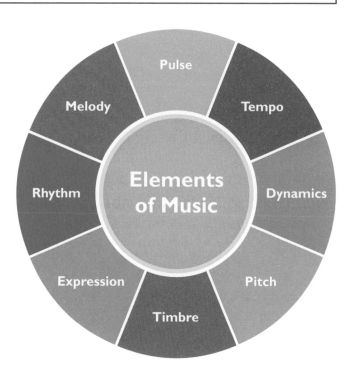

Pulse

A study of the elements of music should always begin with **beat** or **pulse** – the regular, basic unit of evenly repeated time. We tap our feet to it, and musicians often use it when counting themselves in before they play together.

'Beat' is the heart of music! A good place to understand it is to listen to your heart beating in your chest. Sometimes hearing this can be difficult, but you can check your pulse by placing two fingers on the left side of your neck, just under your jaw-bone; you should feel a steady pulse. Tap your foot to this pace, and you will find you have a steady heartbeat.

It may sometimes go faster or slower, but typically our resting heart-rate should be around 60 pulses per minute. To check, first make sure you can feel it. Then look at your watch and count the number of beats in 10 seconds. Multiply this by 6 to get your heart-rate per minute.

Wellbeing

Name: _____ I measured my heart-rate as _____ pulses per minute.

Tapping our feet is something people do all the time when they are listening to or playing music. The pulse or beat of music is easy to find. Even young children can enjoy the pulse of their favourite songs, allowing them to tap, clap or dance along.

 With your teacher's help, identify and listen to two songs or pieces of music in contrasting styles. Listen for the pulse and complete the grid below.

Title	Composer or artist	Describe the pulse

Investigating the pulse or beat of music helps you become more aware of tempo and style – for instance the way a fast pulse sounds in different styles of music.

25

Tempo

Nearly all music has a steady pulse or beat. Did you observe in our listening activity that it can occur at different speeds: fast, moderate or slow? This is called **tempo**.

Tempo is the speed or pace of a piece of music. You will see an indication of the tempo (or speed) at the beginning of most pieces of music, above the first notes. The word 'tempo' means 'time' in Italian, and many other words used to indicate how to play music are also in Italian. This is because Italian composers were the first to write instructions on their music scores. Other composers copied them, also using Italian words, and so Italian became a worldwide language for music, including tempo markings.

A tempo marking is the composer's written indicator of speed. A performer looks at the tempo marking to see how fast or slow to play.

But what do all the words mean? Here are some common Italian words for tempo:

Tempo marking	Translation/Meaning
Andante	Walking pace, easy-going
Adagio	Quite slow
Allegro	Fast
Presto	Very fast
Vivace	Full of life
Moderato	Moderate pace
Largo	Slow
Prestissimo	As fast as possible

 Listen to these two pieces of music and analyse the tempo.

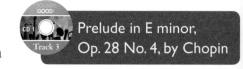
Prelude in E minor, Op. 28 No. 4, by Chopin

Transcribe your findings in the Venn diagram below. A Venn diagram is a way of showing what is shared and what is different.

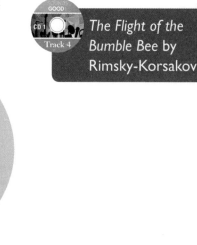
The Flight of the Bumble Bee by Rimsky-Korsakov

Prelude in E minor **The Flight of the Bumble Bee**

Metronome marks

Many composers use **metronome marks** as well as – or even instead of – the Italian terms. Metronome marks allow for more specific control of speed, by stating the desired tempo precisely, in beats per minute (or **BPM**), like this:

The metronome mark tells us the music should have a tempo of 84 crotchet beats per minute. The music is the opening of a piano piece by Béla Bartók, called 'Sorrow'.

To check how fast a piece should be performed, a player or **conductor** uses a metronome. Traditional ones have a clockwork motor, and make a loud regular click, while modern ones are electronic and can be set to flash silently. The metronome is set to the desired tempo, indicating the speed of pulse the composer wants.

With your teacher's help, choose and listen to three songs or pieces of music in a variety of styles. Listen to the tempo and discuss which tempo marking would be suitable. To help you, consult this chart showing the Italian terms and their approximate equivalent in beats per minute. Note that these equivalents are not exact; they depend partly on the character of the music.

Tempo marking	Approximate BPM
Largo	40–66
Adagio	60–76
Andante	76–108
Moderato	100–120
Allegro	120–168
Vivace	132–168
Presto	160–208
Prestissimo	178–208 or more

	Title	Composer or artist	Suitable tempo marking
1			
2			
3			

Activity

Work together to create a short rhythmic pattern that your whole class can clap together. Clap your rhythm pattern at different tempos using a metronome to set the pulse and keep you in time.

Questionnaire

1 Indicate why a composer would want a specific tempo.

_____

_____

2 Propose a suitable type or genre of music that would be more likely to use fast

tempos. _____

3 Apart from slowing down your foot tapping, what effect can slower tempos have

on the listener?

_____

_____

4 Who might help musicians to stay together when playing music at certain speeds?

_____

5 List three Italian words that are used to describe tempo.

_____   _____

_____

What stuck with you?

Evaluate your learning in this
chapter. List what stuck with
you and new key words.

The images below represent something we are familiar with. They are used to change the volume levels on our TVs, phones, computers or stereos.

The levels of sound in music vary from very soft to very loud. Listen to an extract from *The Firebird* by Stravinsky, a colourful ballet based on Russian fairy tales.

 Extract from *The Firebird* by Stravinsky

Complete the following table as you listen.

Can you hear the music clearly at the beginning?	
What tempo would be suitable here?	
Did you notice any changes in volume?	
How did the music make you feel?	
Where would you hear music like this performed?	
Has Stravinsky successfully illustrated an image of the bird for you? Give reasons for your answer.	

In this work we hear many changes in **dynamics**. Stravinsky uses them to bring his composition to life. But how did the musicians know when to play louder or softer?

In written music, dynamic markings indicate how loud or quiet a piece of music should be. Dynamics often change within a piece of music. Once decided by the composer, symbols are written under the stave to indicate what dynamic should be applied by the performer. It is not the same as moving volume levels up or down on your TV remote. If you turned down Stravinsky's *Firebird* on your CD player the dynamic changes would still be there.

The two basic dynamic indications in music are *piano*, meaning softly or quietly, usually abbreviated to *p*; and *forte*, meaning loudly, usually abbreviated to *f*.

Only two options – loud or soft – would be boring, wouldn't it? So there are also symbols for more nuanced dynamics. These are indicated by *mp*, standing for *mezzo-piano* and meaning 'half-quiet'; and *mf*, standing for *mezzo-forte* and meaning 'half-loud'. Composers also use *ff* or *fff* and *pp* or *ppp* for extreme dynamics of loud and soft.

If a composer wants to create a gradual change in dynamics, they can write *crescendo* (or *cresc.*), meaning 'becoming louder', or *diminuendo* (or *dim.*), meaning 'becoming softer'.

Or they can use these symbols, called 'hairpins':

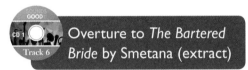

The crescendo hairpin has two lines opening outwards, meaning the music should gradually get louder, and the diminuendo hairpin has two lines closing in, meaning the music should gradually get softer.

 Overture to *The Bartered Bride* by Smetana (extract)
CD 1 Track 6

Listen to the Overture to the opera *The Bartered Bride* by the Czech composer Smetana.

As you listen, look at the chart on the right and point to where you think the dynamics are as the music plays.

Then choose another piece of your own and do the same thing, tracing the **dynamics** on the chart. Discuss with your teacher what would be a suitable piece – one with lots of variation between loud and soft.

Choice of piece:

_____

Performer:

_____

Dynamic facts

◆ Renaissance composer Giovanni Gabrieli was one of the first to indicate dynamics in music notation.

◆ Romantic composer Tchaikovsky sometimes used *ppppp* or *fffff* in his compositions to indicate extremely soft or extremely loud.

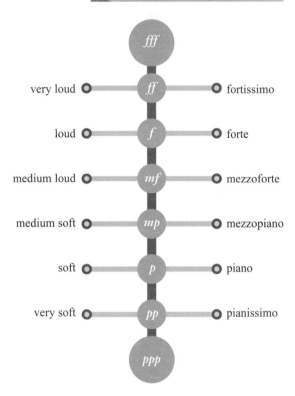

Listen to these melodies on the CD, and look at the notation below, which is just the first phrase of each piece.

◆ For each piece, identify a suitable dynamic and write it in the correct position.

◆ Also, choose a suitable tempo marking and write it above the music.

 'Lullaby' by Brahms
CD 1 Track 7

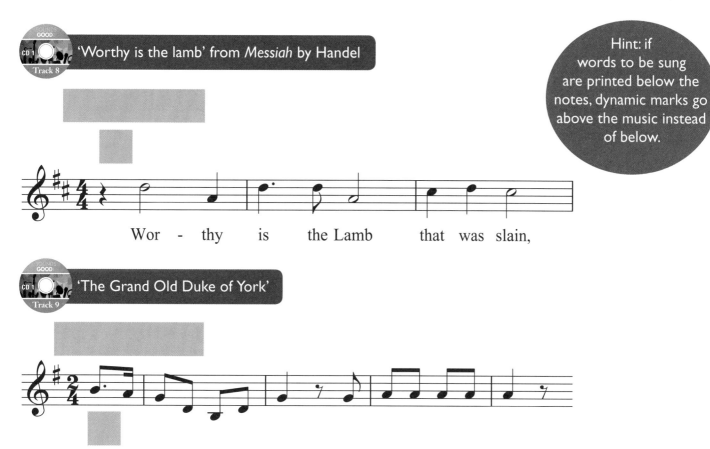

'Worthy is the lamb' from *Messiah* by Handel

Wor - thy is the Lamb that was slain,

Hint: if words to be sung are printed below the notes, dynamic marks go above the music instead of below.

'The Grand Old Duke of York'

Tempo and dynamics are important components of any piece of music. When listening or composing, we should always take time to consider both of these elements. How are they complementing the music or improving the experience for the listener?

 We have looked at lots of new words in covering these topics. Classify these words and their meanings by completing the word bank below.

Word	Meaning	Word	Meaning
forte	loud	allegro	fast

What stuck with you?

Evaluate your learning in this chapter. List what stuck with you and new key words.

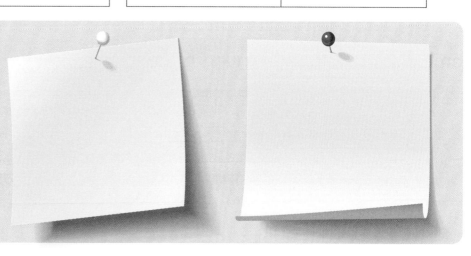

Pitch

Sound

Did you know that every sound we hear is created by something vibrating? The vibrations move through the air and are known as **soundwaves**. Our sensitive eardrums process these vibrations, causing the eardrums to vibrate as well. This process creates nervous impulses which are transmitted to the brain. Our brain identifies and categorises them, and as a result we 'hear' the sounds.

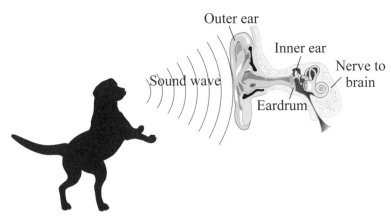

The dog's barking makes vibrations in the air, which are transferred to the eardrum, then recognised by the brain.

High and low sounds

Music uses both high and low sounds to create melodies and harmonies. Our brain works to distinguish the notes it hears, even when there are several at once.

The **pitch** of a note is measured by the frequency of vibration of the soundwave. It is measured in units called **hertz** (Hz), the number of vibrations per second. For instance, the frequency of the note **Middle C** is 256Hz. A soundwave vibrating at 256 vibrations per second creates the note Middle C. Simply, the higher the frequency the higher the sound.

There are two instruments in the picture. Which do you think plays the high notes and which the low ones?

The instrument on the left plays the

_____ notes.

The instrument on the right plays the

_____ notes.

You will learn about these instruments, and many others, in Unit 4. But maybe you already know what they are?

_____ and

_____

Game: Pass the sound around the room

Starting with one person and going round the room, each person sings a note. Choose your own note. Whilst waiting your turn, listen carefully from one sound to the next. As each person sings their note, ask yourself if the pitch has gone up or down.

Repeat this game using other sound sources to illustrate pitch. Explore what sound sources are available to you. A sound source is anything which creates a sound wave. Be creative.

Game: Ten sounds

You will hear ten sounds, 3 seconds apart.
For each sound, decide:

◆ Is it a high or low **pitch**?

◆ Is it higher or lower than the previous sound?

◆ Can you identify or describe the sound source?

As the CD track plays, try to write as much as you can about each sound.

High or low pitch?	Higher or lower than previous sound?	Identify or describe the sound
1		
2		
3		
4		
5		
6		
7		
8		
9		
10		

Pitch facts

◆ The pitch of our voice is controlled by the length of our vocal chords and how fast they vibrate in our voice box.

◆ The human ear can pick up frequencies between about 20Hz and 20,000Hz, but whales can hear lower frequencies than us and dogs can hear higher ones.

Timbre

Pitch helps us to distinguish sounds where one is higher or lower than the other – for instance a dog barking and a bird chirping. But have you ever considered how easily we recognise sounds even when the pitch is not so different? For instance:

◆ Identifying friends or family from their voices alone

◆ Which teacher is making an announcement on the school intercom system

◆ If it's your dog or next door's that's barking outside

◆ If it's wind or rain we hear outside the window

◆ Whether it's Bart or Homer speaking on the TV in the sitting room

◆ If we're listening to a violin or a flute

It's because every sound has a distinct set of characteristics which allows our brain to process and recognise it.

> **Timbre** is the word that describes the tone or colour or **unique quality** of every sound source: voices, instruments and other noises.

Tuning up

Before an orchestra begins to perform, all the musicians 'tune up', playing the note A to make sure they are in tune with each other. This is their tuning note, and its frequency is 440Hz.

Even when all the instruments play the same note, we can hear that there are various different instruments playing. The A on the violin and the A on the flute will sound different.

Classroom orchestra tuning experiment

Gather as many instruments as you can in your classroom, and play the note A on each. It is easy to hear how the timbre varies from one instrument to the next. Likewise, if you play the same notes on a piano and on a guitar, you will clearly hear two different timbres.

Record the result of the tuning experiment on the chart below.

Aim of Experiment:		Date:
Instruments used:	Process (what we did):	
Notes played:	Our findings:	

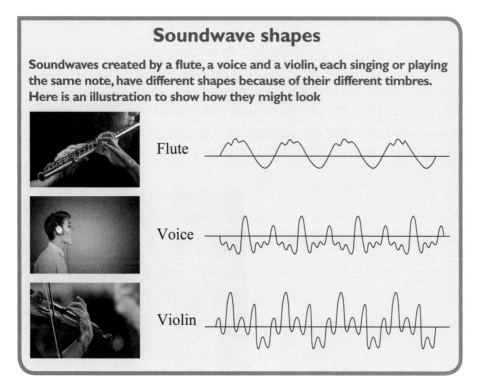

Soundwave shapes

Soundwaves created by a flute, a voice and a violin, each singing or playing the same note, have different shapes because of their different timbres. Here is an illustration to show how they might look

Flute

Voice

Violin

Why is timbre important?

◆ We have many instruments to choose from today. Instruments have been developed and adapted over centuries, expanding the variety of sounds available to us. Therefore composers have many instruments and sounds to choose from when they are composing new music.

◆ Different instruments and sounds can help to convey different emotions or moods.

◆ Carefully chosen instruments or voices can dramatically improve how a melody comes across. Matching the perfect timbre to a melody is an important element of composition.

Now we know what **timbre** means, how do we describe it when discussing what we hear?

Many words are used to describe timbre. If we consider the timbre of a person's voice, we may use words such as nasal, raspy, bright, sharp or warm to describe how it sounds. When talking about instruments, we might say a trumpet is brassy or bright, or that a flute sounds light or delicate. When talking about a cello or double bass we might say the timbre is dark, smooth or mellow.

List other words you can think of that could be used to describe the **timbre** of a sound.

_____   _____   _____

_____   _____   _____

What stuck with you?

Evaluate your learning in this chapter. List what stuck with you and new key words.

Musical scores, as well as including words for **tempo** and **dynamics**, also often include words for **expression**, instructing the performer to play in a way that gives the music a certain feeling or mood. The French composer Poulenc tells pianists to make his *Pavane* sound 'slow and melancholy', the *Toccata* 'very animated' and the *Pastorale* 'calm and mysterious'. In his *War Requiem* Benjamin Britten asks the chorus to sing the Libera me in a 'lamenting' way, whereas the Sanctus should be 'brilliant'.

Mood is the emotion of a piece of music: the feelings evoked or the expressive ability of a piece of music when we listen to it. Mood can also be recognised as the overall atmosphere created by the music. Sometimes we see the different moods of music reflected in the different ways people dance to it.

We use many words to describe mood in music:

Happy	Mysterious
Sad	Scary
Excited	Dark
Relaxed	Cheerful
Tense	Energetic
Calm	Aggressive

Can you list two more words we could use?

_____

_____

_____

_____

Music in marketing

As we go through the day, we experience music in many different places. Sitting on the Luas or bus, getting into a lift, meeting friends in a restaurant or popping into our favourite high street store – nearly always there'll be music in the background.

What we hear isn't just accidental; there are marketing companies all over the world with the job of providing music to create the right 'customer experience' for brands and businesses. Careful consideration is given to which types of music are going to work best in any given setting.

Marketing consultants think about the expression or mood of the music. Researchers are constantly looking for connections between music and human behaviour. The study of moods or emotion in music is called musical psychology.

 Suggest the type of music marketing companies might group into playlists for companies or brands and their customers. Consider the mood the music should convey, and choose a suitable example of music that could be played. Work together to complete the research box below.

Place	Song/Composition	Reasons for your choice
Sports shop		
Hotel lift		
Restaurant		
Waiting room		
Toyshop		

Playlist for a business

Compile a **playlist** of five songs which you feel would provide a suitable mood or atmosphere in one of the business premises listed above.

Place/Premises	
Artist	**Title**
1	
2	
3	
4	
5	

Emotion in music

The **mood** of music can affect us deeply. It makes us feel varied and complex emotions. Listen to these two pieces of classical music and decide what mood the composer is creating or how they make you feel. Then, with your teacher, decide on a third piece of your own choice, in whatever style you like, add it to the chart below.

Mood or feeling:

'The Swan' from *Carnival of the Animals* by Saint-Saëns

Mood or feeling:

The Liberty Bell (march) by Sousa

(your choice) Title:

Mood or feeling:

What stuck with you?

Evaluate your learning in this chapter. List what stuck with you and new key words.

Melody

Melody is a word we are familiar with; we understand that it is the central component of a piece of music. A melody we like can get stuck in our head for days!

Melody is a combination of **pitch** and **rhythm**. It is always moving, using rhythm patterns to keep in time with the pulse. A melody groups pitches (higher or lower sounds) in a way that creates a musical idea or motif.

What words can we use to describe the melodies we hear?
Words often used to describe melody include:

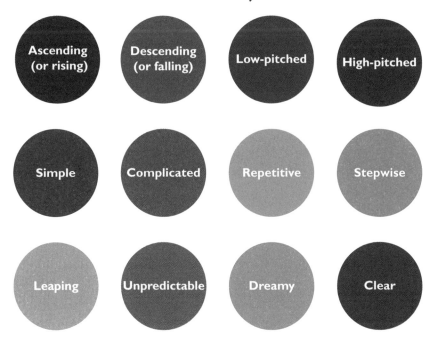

Ascending (or rising)   Descending (or falling)   Low-pitched   High-pitched

Simple   Complicated   Repetitive   Stepwise

Leaping   Unpredictable   Dreamy   Clear

Can you suggest two more descriptive words for melody?

_____

_____

With your teacher, choose five songs or pieces of music in a variety of styles. Listen carefully to the melodies, including the rhythm patterns they use, and think about how you would describe them.

No.	Title	Describe the melody line
1		
2		
3		
4		
5		

Rhythm

When we describe the **rhythm** of a piece of music, we are talking about patterns of long and short sounds and of silences, within the music.

Earlier in this unit we learned about **pulse** or beat. It is important to understand that pulse is not the same as rhythm. The rhythmic patterns in music are *built* on the beat, but they can divide or go across the beat.

Rhythm is written onto sheet music using note values which represent how long or short each sound should be; we'll learn more about this later!

To help identify the difference between pulse and rhythm, try this experiment:

1 Choose a piece of music to listen to.

2 Allow your foot to tap to the pulse.

3 Then attempt to clap the rhythm of the song with your hands, while continuing to tap your foot to the pulse.

Rhythm games

 Try the following activities together in groups.

1 Taking turns, clap the rhythm pattern of your full name. Listen to the pattern and try to describe it. Then clap the rhythm of another person in your group and see if your friends can recognise whose name you are clapping.

You may notice that you tend to emphasise some claps more than others. This is your in-built metronome telling you how the rhythm you are clapping fits in with the pulse or beat.

2 Staying in your group, form a circle. The first person should clap a short rhythm pattern. Each person in your group claps the same rhythm in turn, passing it on to the next person. This forms a repeated rhythm pattern or **ostinato**, something we will learn more about later.

Continue until each person has had a turn, then try another pattern. Then try applying a faster or slower **tempo**, or using a louder or softer **dynamic**.

We will learn more about rhythm later. For now, consider some words we can use to describe the rhythm patterns we hear in the music we are listening to.

 Discuss the words in the wheel used to describe rhythm.

 With your teacher, choose five songs or pieces of music in a variety of styles. Listen carefully to identify the rhythm patterns in the music, and think about how you would describe them.

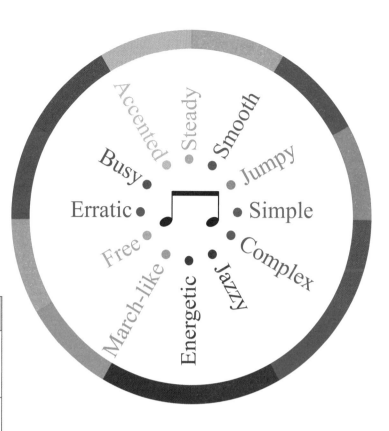

No.	Title	Describe the rhythm
1		
2		
3		
4		
5		

What stuck with you?

Evaluate your learning in this chapter. List what stuck with you and new key words.

Reflection and Evaluation Sheet

Unit title:

Music I listened to:

Learning and exploring

I really enjoyed…

Something interesting I learned…

I excelled at…

My biggest challenge was…

I overcame this by…

I would like to learn more about…

New key words

Skills I developed in this unit…

This unit reminded me of learning about…

Goal setting…

-
-
-

Rate your learning

The Listening Lab

In this unit

*Music is a source of understanding history. In this unit you will discover that music often reflects the time or era when it was composed. Listening to and appraising music from different historical periods will improve your skills of analysis, comparison and evaluation, develop your musical vocabulary and demonstrate your understanding of the **elements of music**. You will use your new knowledge to help you to accurately identify and define the expressive qualities which feature in musical works in this unit. You will collaborate with others to imagine and create music. Together you will develop your ideas and present your creation to your classmates. You will develop research skills necessary for completion of your CBA2. An ability to research and evaluate the background information, inspiration or intentions of composers and the historical context of a piece of music is essential in order to write a programme note.*

Intended learning

Illustrate the structure of a piece of music through a physical or visual representation.

1.11, 1.14, 3.2 3.3, 3.6, 3.7 CBA2

Compare pieces of music that are similar in period and style by different composers from different countries.

Examine and interpret the impact of music on the depiction of characters, their relationships and their emotions, as explored in instrumental music of different genres.

Make a study of a particular contemporary or historical musical style, analyse its structures and use of musical devices, and describe the influence of other styles on it.

What is listening?

Listening is a skill that is vital to communication. The ability to listen and interpret information is very important. It is one of the first communication skills we develop in life: we must listen before we can develop the skills which allow us to speak, read or write.

Hearing is not quite the same as **listening**. Many people passively hear music: they sit back and let it drift over them. They may be enjoying the music, but they don't recognise anything in particular happening.

Listening is different: when we listen we concentrate on the sounds we hear and process these into knowledge. This is known as **active listening**. It develops our aural skills, helping us to listen more effectively, especially to speech, music or natural sounds.

What is art?

Music is one of the arts. But what is art?

Art is the creation of something beautiful or meaningful using skill and imagination. The word 'art' comes from the Latin word *ars*, which means art, skill or craft – not just a painting or sculpture but anything of beauty or value which has been created using creativity and imagination. Literature, dance, music, visual arts and theatre are all valued types of art.

The house called *Falling Water*, by architect Frank Lloyd Wright

 Argue the benefits of the arts for our wellbeing.

_____

_____

As individuals, art affects us in different ways. Walking through an art gallery, you may be drawn to one particular painting, and the books you like most might not be enjoyed by your friends. In the same way, when we listen carefully to music it affects each of us in different ways. Our individual response to a piece of music is unique to us.

Ballerina Margot Fonteyn

How does music affect *you*?

_____

_____

Actor John Gielgud as Richard the Third

Hungarian composer Gyorgy Ligeti

Writer Roddy Doyle

Portrait of Monet by Renoir

Responding to a piece of music through another art-form

Listen to 'La Mer' by Debussy and, using any materials and colours available to you, draw whatever picture pops into your head or reflects how the piece of music makes you feel. Maybe it reminds you of raindrops or of being in a boat on the water, riding a bike, relaxing, dancing or spending time with someone. Your response may not be a clear image: it may be washes of colour or shapes. Alternatively, be a **choreographer**: create a dance that you think is a reflection of the music.

 Listen to the music as you work on your painting or your dance. Once completed, share your creation with the class. You may be surprised by the varied responses to the music shown in each other's work.

Debussy wrote 'I love the sea and I have listened to it passionately.' Critique Debussy's ability to illustrate the image of the sea in this piece of music

What stuck with you?

Evaluate your learning in this chapter. List what stuck with you and new key words.

In the rest of this unit we will study music of various styles and periods, and investigate how the different elements of music are used by composers when creating their works. We will also learn about two more elements, **texture** and **form**.

Before we begin, let's recap what we already know from the previous unit. Can you remember the elements of music we discussed there, and what they meant?

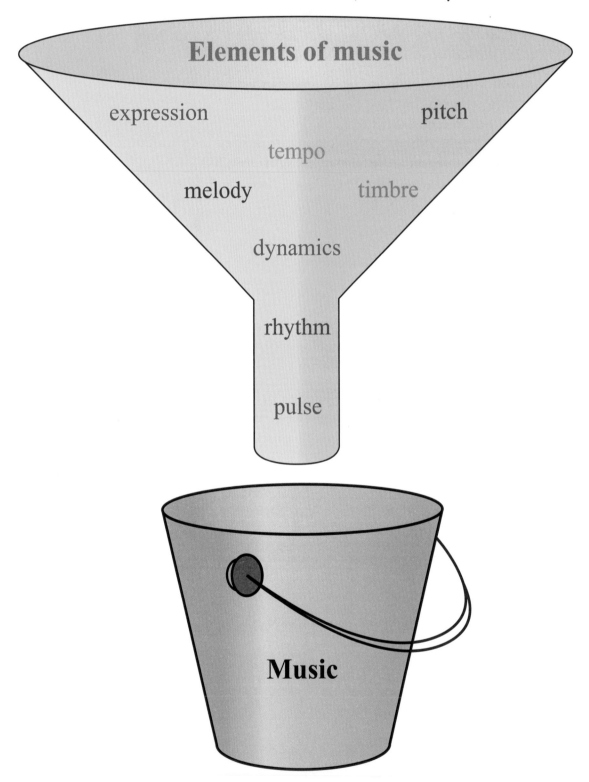

Active listening 1: The Confrontation

'The Confrontation' from *Les Misérables* by Claude-Michel Schönberg

Work in pairs to recognise the key musical elements and how they are mixed together.

◆ Looking at the grid below, tick the box beside each element you can identify.

◆ Discuss what you heard with your partner, and report your findings.

◆ Space has been left for you to add any other points of interest you noticed in the piece.

Expression	☐
Tempo	☐
Dynamics	☐
Rhythm	☐
Melody	☐
Any other points of interest included:	

Active listening 2: Your choice

In collaboration with your teacher, make your own choice of piece to listen to.

Then, in just the same way as before, listen for the musical elements and use the grid to describe how they are used.

Title	
Composer or singer	
Genre	
Expression	☐
Tempo	☐
Dynamics	☐
Rhythm	☐
Melody	☐
Any other points of interest included:	

What stuck with you?

Evaluate your learning in this chapter. List what stuck with you and new key words.

Have you looked at timelines in your other lessons? A timeline is used to sequence events along a line. It gives a clear picture of when things happened and in what order. A music timeline shows us the different periods in the history of music. All of the forms of art we read about earlier have similar periods of history on their timelines. Look at the music timeline below.

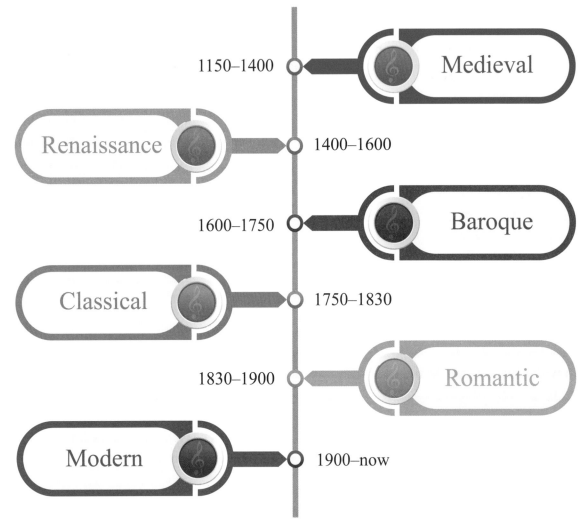

1150–1400 — Medieval

Renaissance — 1400–1600

1600–1750 — Baroque

Classical — 1750–1830

1830–1900 — Romantic

Modern — 1900–now

We will compare the music of these eras by **actively listening** to music written by composers from each period.

 Try to do some research on each era, its composers and their music. Each era is recognisable in its own way. It is distinguished by the instruments available, and the types of sounds that were preferred by composers of that time. Include some research on the literature, architecture, paintings and other art forms of that time. You may find some interesting connections between them.

In this unit we will focus on music from the main eras that musicians tend to perform nowadays: Baroque, Classical, Romantic and Modern.

What defines each period? That's an interesting question we will explore together as we experience music from these eras in the next few pages!

Active listening 3: Galliard Battaglia

Galliard Battaglia by Samuel Scheidt

Listen to this piece of music by the German composer Samuel Scheidt (1587–1654). How would you describe it? What images come into your mind when you listen to it?

As you might guess, a *galliard battaglia* is a 'gallant battle'. Do you think Scheidt was successful in creating a piece of music which **illustrates** a gallant battle? It was composed for an **ensemble** of cornetts, predecessors of our present-day brass instruments. It is performed here by two trumpets, horn, trombone and tuba. It was composed in the early 1600s and belongs to the early **Baroque** period. Look back at our music timeline to check the dates.

Consort of cornetts (not to be confused with the present-day brass cornet)

 Listen to the relationship between the two trumpets. Scheidt has written their parts to illustrate the two sides in the battle, echoing and competing with each other.

Listen to the music again and complete the grid below as you listen.

 Use this form as a template for appraising pieces of music in this chapter, especially the way the elements of music are used.

Title
Composer
Era (period)
Instrumentation
Expression or mood
Tempo
Dynamics
Rhythm
Melody
Any other points of interest

Baroque music

The Baroque era spans from 1600 to 1750. It was an important time for the world. Great thinkers like Galileo and Newton were making important discoveries about the universe. In music, art, literature and architecture inspiration came from decoration and embellishment. Music, like architecture, was rich in ornamentation.

Composers worked under **patronage**, usually of the church or aristocratic households. Research the word *patronage* and note your findings below.

_____

_____

Composers under patronage were often given direction as to what they should compose. Would this have limited their creative freedom?

Many Baroque composers wrote music for the dances popular at that time. **Suites** are sets of dances, and many suites from the Baroque era remain popular today. Research the word *suite*, and define this popular form from the Baroque era.

_____

_____

You have listened to a piece by the German composer Samuel Scheidt. Other composers from the Baroque era include Bach, Handel, Monteverdi, Purcell and Vivaldi. Choose one, investigate their life and music and interpret your research below. Name a piece of music by your chosen composer and mention why you like it.

_____

_____

_____

_____

Instruments in the Baroque era

In the Baroque period, the piano had not yet been invented. Other keyboard instruments were used, including the harpsichord. Do some research into this instrument and indicate your findings below. Distinguish the differences between a harpsichord and a piano.

_____

_____

_____

_____

_____

_____

Active listening 4: 'Pantomime' from *Les Petits Riens* by Mozart

 'Pantomime' from *Les Petits Riens* by Mozart

Les Petits Riens ('Little Nothings') was a ballet with music by Mozart. It was performed in Paris in 1778 but was a failure, and Mozart's manuscript was lost until the late 1800s.

 Listen carefully to how the melody moves – sometimes up, sometimes down, sometimes smooth, sometimes jumping abruptly. Composers try to keep their listeners interested by varying the way the melody moves.

While listening, follow the upward or downward movement of the melody with your arm. Sometimes the movement is gradual, and sometimes it moves all the way up or down in **ascending** or **descending scales**.

 Listen again, and complete the chart below.

Title	
Composer	
Era (period)	
Instrumentation	
Expression or mood	
Tempo	
Dynamics	
Rhythm	
Melody	
Any other points of interest	

Les Petits Riens is a **ballet**. Research this form and compose a note on it below.

_____

_____

_____

Mozart

Mozart is one of greatest of all composers. His music belongs to the **Classical** era. Many history books refer to him as a child prodigy; he composed prolifically from a young age and performed for royalty by the age of six. He was brilliant at remembering what he had heard, and his talent for writing music developed quickly; he composed a Missa Brevis by the age of twelve, and completed over six hundred works in his short life. He died in 1791 aged only 36. His work encompassed every possible type of music from solo piano pieces and all sorts of chamber music to concertos and symphonies, church music and operas.

Mozart playing music with his father and sister

Maria Anna Mozart

Mozart's older sister, Maria Anna, was also a talented musician. Investigate her life, and discover what you can about her. Discuss what it was like to be a female musician at that time.

As a classical composer Mozart belonged to an era of composers who wrote in a balanced and clear style, less elaborate than the Baroque composers before and not as outwardly emotional as the Romantic composers who followed.

The balanced style of classical music can be heard in its melodic phrases. Listen to *Les Petits Riens* again and notice that the **pulse** is steady throughout. There are 16 beats in each **phrase** or musical sentence. While listening, count the beats; you should hear a new phrase begin after 16 beats.

Phrases

A phrase is like a musical sentence. There are three phrases in 'Twinkle twinkle little star'. Sing it together, and see if you can identify where each new phrase begins.

Music in the Classical period

The **Classical** era in music is the period from 1750 to 1830. Compared with the Baroque period, classical music is recognised by its lighter texture. A clear and pronounced melody was important to the classical composers, and they were less interested in weaving many melodies together.

 You have listened to a piece by Mozart. Other famous composers from this era include Haydn, Gluck, Boccherini and Beethoven. Choose one, investigate their life and music. Demonstrate evidence of your research below. Name a piece of music by your chosen composer and mention why you like it.

_____

_____

_____

Haydn and Mozart knew and admired each other, and both were a big influence on the younger Beethoven. However, Beethoven's music developed radically, becoming larger in scale and more dramatic – so much so that we consider his music to mark the transition from Classical to Romantic music.

Instruments and ensembles at this time

Many developments were made with instruments in this period. The **orchestra** acquired its standard recognisable form, with strings, woodwind, brass and percussion; we will learn more about this in the next unit. As the orchestra grew, composers enjoyed more choice of tone and **timbre**. The string quartet, likewise, became a standard chamber music ensemble, with two violins, viola and cello. The harpsichord had been the main keyboard instrument in the Baroque period, but by 1800 it was superseded by the piano.

Haydn

 Sonatas, **symphonies** and **concertos** were popular forms used by the classical composers. Research these, and write a description of them below.

Sonata: _____

_____

Symphony: _____

_____

Concerto: _____

_____

Broadwood piano from 1808

Active listening 5: *The Sleeping Beauty* by Tchaikovsky

 'The Blue Bird and Princess Florine' from *The Sleeping Beauty* by Tchaikovsky.

This piece of music was written by Russian composer Tchaikovsky for the ballet *The Sleeping Beauty*. This section of the work is called 'The Blue Bird and Princess Florine', two fairytale characters who feature in the final act of the ballet. They appear along with other well-known fairytale characters including Puss-in-Boots and Little Red Riding Hood.

 As you listen to this piece, close your eyes and imagine you are dancing in a ballet. You might even do a pirouette!

The music opens with a song-like melody on the flute, during which the character Florine cups her hand to her ear; almost as though she were listening to the Blue Bird singing to her from outside the castle. The story comes from a French fairytale, *L'Oiseau bleu* ('The Blue Bird'). It is a story of true love: the Blue Bird is her beloved Prince, changed by a spell and forbidden from marrying her. As the story comes to an end, true love prevails and the two are married and live … can you guess?

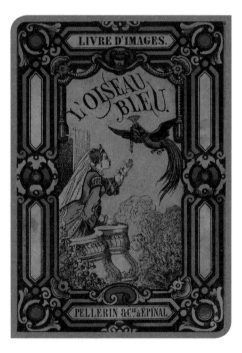

Tchaikovsky, like many Romantic composers, paid great attention to **illustrating** stories and emotions through their music. Characters were often represented by their own melody – which could be as long or short as the composer desired, moving away from the balance and structure of the Classical era. Large orchestras were used to create varied **moods**, **textures** and **timbres** in an attempt to move audiences emotionally.

 Points of interest for you to listen out for and discuss:

◆ Why, do you think, did Tchaikovsky choose the flute for the Blue Bird's romantic melody at the beginning? Propose another suitable instrument for this part.

◆ It is clear from the music that there are two characters in this story. (In ballet terms, the dance is called a 'pas de deux'. What does that mean?) The flute melody begins the **dialogue** between these two characters. Does the music continue to **illustrate** this conversation? How does Tchaikovsky achieve this?

Listen again to 'The Blue Bird and Princess Florine', and evaluate how the elements of music are used by completing the chart in the way you have with the previous pieces.

Title	
Composer	
Era (period)	
Instrumentation	
Expression or mood	
Tempo	
Dynamics	
Rhythm	
Melody	
Any other points of interest	

Research

1 Where was Tchaikovsky born? _____

2 Identify another Romantic composer from a different country.

    _____

3 What are the dates of the Romantic era? _____

4 Describe the orchestra as used by Romantic composers.

    _____

5 Research the following words:

    Incidental Music _____

    Programme Music _____

    Illustrative music _____

6 Name two other **ballets** with music composed by Tchaikovsky.

    _____

    _____

Romantic music

Romantic music? Is it music all about love? Well, it could be, but it could also be about all sorts of other things. Romantic music is all about feelings and emotions. The Romantic composers wanted to express their feelings in their music, and to compose music that would evoke similar emotions in the listener. Beethoven's desire to write music full of feeling would have shocked the first listeners. He displayed his new style of composing in his Symphony No. 3, the 'Eroica' or Heroic Symphony.

The names of female composers are largely missing from text books and standard repertoires before the twentieth century. In the Romantic era, female composers began to make their mark – for instance Fanny Mendelssohn, Clara Schumann – but they were not given the credit their music deserved. Investigate the treatment of female composers and the possible reasons for their absence from the history books. How has the situation for female composers changed since then?

Romantic composers

Research the Romantic composers listed below to find what country they are from and complete information box below.

Composer	Dates	Country of birth	Information on the composer and their work
Mendelssohn	1809–1847		
Chopin			
Schumann			
Liszt			
Tchaikovsky			
Mahler			

Identify two Romantic composers of different nationalities. Choose a piece of music composed by each, and compare and contrast them. Report your findings below:

Composer: _____   Composer: _____

Piece 1: _____   Piece 2: _____

_____   _____

_____   _____

_____   _____

Which piece did you prefer and why?

_____

Programme music

Romantic composers often chose to **illustrate** stories, characters or images in their music. This is known as **programme music**. It aims to tell a story through the music.

In programme music a short melody or tune can be used to represent a **theme** or **character** in the piece. It often recurs or develops as the story proceeds. **Tempo** and **dynamics** are varied as needed to tell the story. Direct imitation of sounds such as birdsong or thunder could be illustrated using instruments.

Writing a programme note

Write a programme note for 'The Blue Bird and Princess Florine' or another Romantic work of your choice. Research the story or emotion being shared by the composer.

Your programme note should include the following:

A brief introduction to the composer
Something about the story told in the music
The circumstances surrounding the composition and why the composer chose to write this music
The voices or instruments involved
What was happening in the composer's country at the time of the composition
Interesting musical signposts to listen out for
Your favourite section of the piece, and why

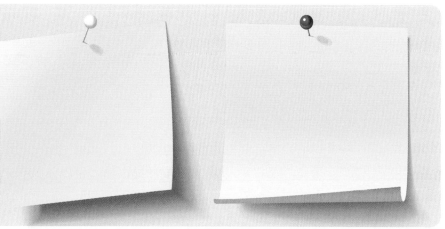

What stuck with you?

Evaluate your learning in this chapter. List what stuck with you and new key words.

Before we continue with the timeline and explore the next era, Modern music, we need to look at two important aspects of how the elements of music are put together: **texture** and **form**.

First, in this chapter we'll examine what **texture** means in music.

If we look up the word 'texture' in a dictionary we will find definitions like:

> The texture of something is the way that it feels when you touch it, for example how smooth or rough it is.
>
> Texture is the visual and tactile quality of a surface.

Consider the texture of what you are wearing, and think how you would describe it. Texture is frequently used to describe things we can touch, like clothes or other materials such as sand, gravel, wood, liquids and foods.

In your art classes, you may have discussed texture when studying pieces of art or artists' techniques. In Van Gogh's painting 'Fishing Boats by the Sea' there are wind-blown grains of sand lying within the paint, and these add to the thick, grainy texture of Van Gogh's style.

Vincent Van Gogh 'Fishing Boats by the Sea'

What is texture in music?

When we describe the **texture** of a piece of music, we are trying to explain how much is going on in the music, how the melodies and harmonies interact.

Texture describes how many **layers** there are in the music and what the role of each layer is. Layers or melodies – lines of music – can be created by singers, instruments or a combination of the two. We can describe music that has many combined melodic parts as having a thick texture and music that has few parts or a single melody as having a thin texture.

The texture of a piece of music can change within a performance: it may begin in one texture and move freely to another. A good question to ask yourself when you listen to a piece of music is: how many melodies (or 'lines' or 'parts') do I hear, and how do they work together?

There are three main types of texture in music:

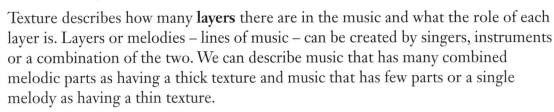

Monophonic   Homophonic   Polyphonic

from the Greek prefixes *mono* (single), *homo* (together), *poly* (many)

On the following pages we will examine these.

Monophony

Monophonic literally means 'one voice'. It is the simplest form of texture as it has only one layer or melody. When we sing our national anthem together we are singing a monophonic line, as we all sing one **melody** together. This is also true when we sing 'Happy Birthday' to a friend. When we are all singing the same melody, we are singing **in unison**.

A group or crowd of singers, singing in unison, is also an example of monophony

Equally, a solo singer or a solo instrument playing without accompaniment are both examples of monophony.

Sometimes a melodic line is represented by a drawn line, outlining how the music flows.

← Melody

This line represents one clear melodic line. There is no accompaniment of any sort.

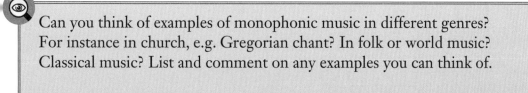

Can you think of examples of monophonic music in different genres? For instance in church, e.g. Gregorian chant? In folk or world music? Classical music? List and comment on any examples you can think of.

_____

_____

_____

Listen to this example.

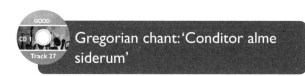
Gregorian chant: 'Conditor alme siderum'

Homophony

Homophony is the most common texture in the music we listen to today. It is defined by having one principal layer or melody, which stands out against a **harmony** or accompanying layer in the background. One part is the main melody, the rest is an **accompaniment**, even if it involves several instruments. The accompaniment typically consists mainly of **chords**, giving a harmonic background, and (in pop and jazz) a rhythm section marking the beat.

Try to recall your favourite pop song in your head. Chances are, you mostly hear the vocalist singing the lyrics of the song, but normally there are also instruments and backing vocals. The vocalist stands out with the main melody, while the other performers add harmony and rhythm.

It is important to understand that the number of people or instruments playing doesn't define the texture. A pianist can play homophonic music, with the melody in the right hand and chords in the left. A large choir singing the melody in unison,

Adele performing at the Tabernacle in London, 2011: melody plus accompaniment

accompanied by an equally large orchestra playing the chords, is also homophonic music. The sound may be very different, but the **texture** is essentially the same.

Do you remember how we could draw a picture of monophonic music? By drawing a single line representing, roughly at least, how the pitch goes up and down. Here's how we could represent homophonic music in a similar manner:

← Melody

← Harmonic accompaniment

The main melody is represented by the flowing line, and the lines underneath represent the chords and rhythm in the accompaniment.

In pairs or groups, identify three examples of homophonic music in **different genres**.

1 _____

2 _____

3 _____

Polyphony

Polyphony literally means 'many sounds'. Polyphonic music is where two or more layers or melodies of <u>equal importance</u> are woven together <u>simultaneously</u>. Polyphonic writing can be complex, and the texture may sound thick to listen to. It can be hard to follow, as each of the melodies or layers are competing for your attention.

Listen to these two examples of polyphony.

 'The Confrontation' from *Les Misérables* by Claude-Michel Schönberg

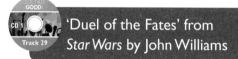 'Duel of the Fates' from *Star Wars* by John Williams

A common form of polyphony is **imitation**. Imitative polyphony uses the <u>same melody</u> in each layer, but at <u>different times</u>, so that the tune seems to be thrown from one part to another. Listen to this example from Handel's *Messiah*, which was first performed in Dublin in 1742.

 'His yoke is easy' from *Messiah* by Handel

How could we represent polyphonic music diagramatically? How about this? Three different melodies sound at the same time.

And this would be a way of picturing imitative polyphony. The same tune comes in successively in four different parts:

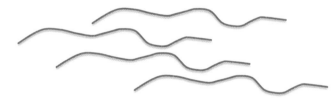

With your teacher, do some research into polyphonic music, and list some examples below.

_____

_____

_____

Different textures in notation

How do **monophony**, **homophony** and **polyphony** appear in notation? Here is the tune 'Row, row, row your boat' presented in three different ways. Work together to rehearse a performance of these three textures using this well-known nursery rhyme.

 First, the tune by itself. This is **monophony**.

Secondly, with a simple **chordal accompaniment**. This is **homophony**.

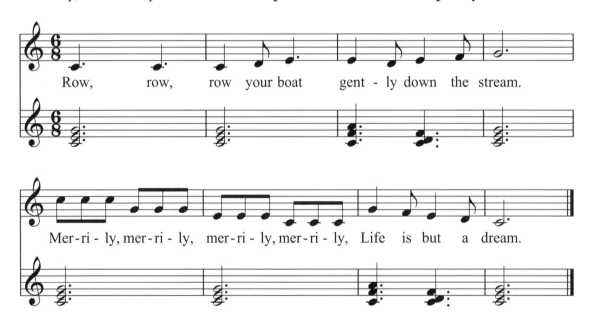

Thirdly, as a three-part vocal **round**. This is **polyphony**; in fact it is **imitative** polyphony.

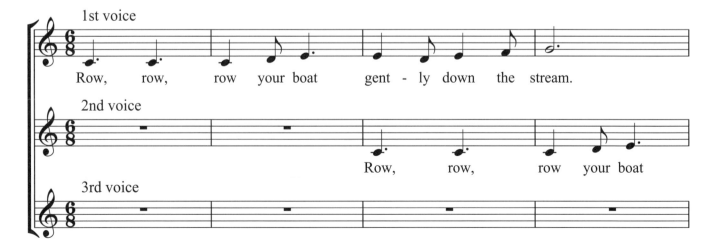

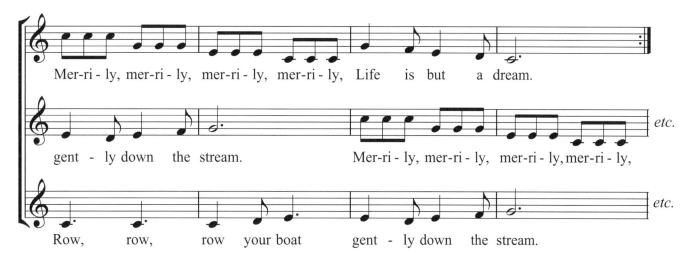

Mer-ri-ly, mer-ri-ly, mer-ri-ly, mer-ri-ly, Life is but a dream.

gent-ly down the stream. Mer-ri-ly, mer-ri-ly, mer-ri-ly, mer-ri-ly, *etc.*

Row, row, row your boat gent-ly down the stream. *etc.*

You can sing it, noticing how the parts enter in turn and how no two parts have the same melody simultaneously.

Identifying different textures

 With your teacher, choose five songs or pieces of music from varied styles. Listen carefully to identify the texture of the music. Remember, texture can often change within the piece.

No.	Title	Describe the texture
1		
2		
3		
4		
5		

Texture is often explained using visual graphics. Design images to illustrate the three textures we have studied.

Monophony	
Homophony	
Polyphony	

How composers used texture in the different musical eras

Renaissance and **Baroque** composers often used polyphony when writing their music. The example on the previous page, from *Messiah*, is typical of Handel's style. Bach, too, wrote much polyphonic music including his 48 Preludes and Fugues, the *Well-tempered Clavier* for keyboard, nowadays often played on the piano. A **fugue** uses imitative polyphony extensively, with the different parts or voices entering with the main tune many times, at different pitches.

 Canon was a similar **composing technique** much used in this era. Research canon, and explain how it was used by Baroque composers to create polyphonic music.

_____

_____

_____

The texture of **classical** music is often homophonic: an easily recognisable main melody with an accompaniment typically based on chords. In fact the easiest way to distinguish classical music from baroque is its lighter texture.

However, we should not generalise too much. All types of musical texture can be found in the music of all periods. Bach and Handel wrote plenty of homophonic music – the opening of the 'Hallelujah Chorus' is an example. Similarly, Mozart and Haydn wrote plenty of polyphonic music in the classical era – especially when they wished to express their admiration for Bach and Handel!

Romantic composers often used texture to help to **illustrate** the story, **mood** or emotion central to their work. **Listen** again to 'The Blue Bird and Princess Florine', CD1 track 26, and describe the texture of this piece and how it reflects the story of Florine and the Blue Bird.

_____

_____

What stuck with you?

Evaluate your learning in this chapter. List what stuck with you and new key words.

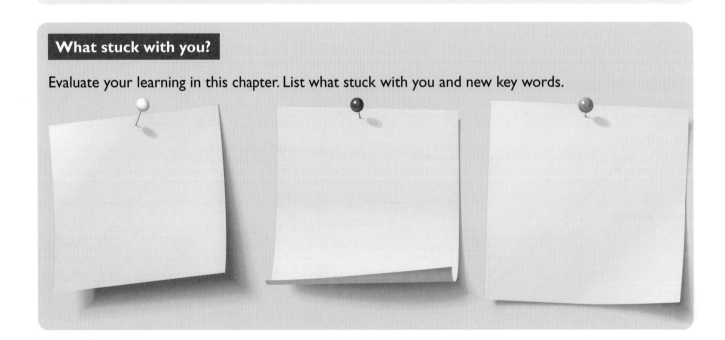

Texture is one important aspect of the way composers organise their musical elements – the melodies, rhythms, timbres, dynamics, etc.

Another equally important aspect is **form**. This is the way the music is structured as it proceeds from the start to the end of a piece – <u>what happens in what order</u>.

To illustrate this idea, let's listen to another piece.

'The Viennese Musical Clock' by Kodály

This piece portrays a musical clock – a large clock with a mechanical action attached, so that when the clock chimes, music begins to play and various model figures, typically soldiers, make ornate movements across the front of the clock. Have you ever seen one?

Before we listen to how Kodály sets this to music, how would you do it? Think about the sounds that a clock makes. Create the tick-tock sound on your desk, using your pointer finger and thumb. You may notice that you tend to emphasise one sound, the 'tick', over the other, the 'tock'. Why might this happen? Then don't forget the chimes that large clocks make on the hour. How might you incorporate that sound into your music?

'The Viennese Musical Clock' from the *Háry János Suite* by Kodály

 Listen to Kodály's music, and try to identify the mechanical movements of a clock illustrated in the music. It opens with rhythmic chiming, played on tubular bells, announcing the change of the hour, followed by a march-like tune during which we can imagine the soldiers appearing through one door and leaving through the one on the other side. This melody returns again and again.

To illustrate this, Kodály has used a structure or form known as **rondo form**.

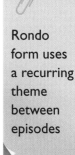
Rondo form uses a recurring theme between episodes

Rondo form can be represented it by the diagram below.

Intro | RECURRING THEME A | B | A | C | A | D | A | Coda

The **Intro** is the tubular bell chimes heard at the start. Then the march tune is represented by the yellow triangle, **A**. It soon becomes familiar, as it returns several times through the piece. It is used by Kodály to tie the music together. It keeps coming round: hence 'rondo'.

In between each hearing of **A** we hear a new melody. Each of these is different and so is represented by different letters: **B**, **C** and **D**. These sections are called **episodes**. Finally there's an end section or **Coda**, with **fanfares** to round off the piece.

Can you see how the diagram represents the musical structure? Letters are often used as a shorthand to describe musical forms. **Listen** to the piece again, moving your finger across the diagram as you hear each refrain or episode appear.

Creating a piece of music with dance or mime to reflect rondo form

Set yourselves into groups of four. Choose one person to be **A** and the remaining three team members to identify as **B, C** and **D**. Collaborate to compose a physical representation of **rondo form** to present to your classmates.

Start by creating a short musical statement for each person. This can be a rhythmic pattern or a melody, or something distinctive of your own. Then try them in the rondo sequence:

A B A C A D A

Then, for each section, think about what the other three team members will do, musically or in movement. Person A will obviously be busy musically, but B, C and D can collaborate to enhance the A sections.

In the box below, summarise your experience. Include information about how you planned your presentation, what each person's role was, what challenges you faced, and evaluate what went well.

Identifying form

Collaborate to identify the form of 'Twinkle twinkle little star'.

1 Identify the phrases. How many are there?

2 Which are the same as each other and which are different?

3 Give each phrase a letter, and enter the letters in the box below.

> A

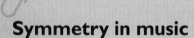

Symmetry in music

Form in music often involves some kind of symmetry, as it does in architecture. Can you hear that 'Twinkle twinkle' has a type of symmetrical structure?

 Research and <u>define</u> the following terms:

Harmony _____

Accompaniment _____

Chords _____

Unison _____

Round _____

Canon _____

Composing Technique _____

Fanfare _____

Kodály

Zoltán Kodály (1882–1967) was a Hungarian composer. As well as his compositions, he left a remarkable legacy in two ways. He was devoted to preserving the folk music of his country, travelling to remote areas to listen to and notate the music of local villagers, ensuring that the music of his people would be written into history forever. Secondly, Kodály was very interested in the music education of young people. This inspired him to reform music education in Hungary, creating the 'Kodály Method' (still practised in many countries). You may recognise these hand signs from your music classes in primary school.

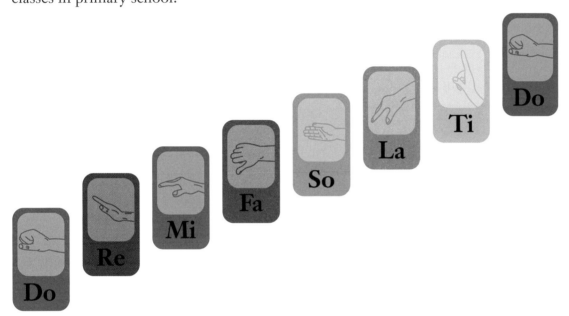

◆ Sing together while you perform the actions, first **ascending** then **descending**.

◆ Compose a short tune using these sounds. Rehearse and perform it, making the hand signs as you sing.

Music maps

A diagram that represents the **structure** or **form** of a piece of music, like the one that we used for Kodály's 'The Viennese Musical Clock', is called a musical map. We can follow it while we listen to the music; it guides us through.

There are other things you can bring into a music map, like **texture**. Earlier in this unit we looked at how different types of musical texture – monophonic, homophonic, polyphonic – could be represented in diagrams (see pages 59, 60 and 61). Also, you can incorporate a **timeline** into a music map, marking the timings at which different things in the music happen. Whenever a piece has a clear structure, we could make a music map of it that we can follow while listening.

Look again at the music map of 'The Viennese Musical Clock' on page 65. Letters and shapes represent the different sections of the rondo, with **A** being the section that keeps coming round, and we have added a box for the Intro and another for the Coda (ending). Listen again while you follow the music map.

 Now listen to the previous piece we studied, Tchaikovsky's 'The Blue Bird and Princess Florine' CD 1 track 26. How could that be represented as a music map? As you listen, think about out what form it takes, what happens, section by section. Revise and illustrate this piece of music in a music map.

Be creative in how you do it – for instance how one instrument is joined by another as the piece progresses, and if necessary include a key to explain the different shapes or symbols you have used. Listen to the music as you work.

Graphic scores

In the mid-twentieth century composers began to take this idea a stage further and developed **graphic scores**. These differ from music maps in one important way: a **score** is what the musicians actually play from, whereas a music map is just a representation of the piece. We will learn more about graphic scores later in this book and look at some examples.

Modern Music

Kodály's 'The Viennese Musical Clock' is a piece from the modern era of music, and on the next page we introduce the 'Golliwogg's Cakewalk' by Debussy. You may remember listening to the *Firebird Suite* by Stravinsky, which we met on page 29. Composers like Stravinsky and Debussy were interested in breaking away from the mood and style of the Romantic era, and in creating new, more modern sounds.

In later units we will investigate more recent composers, and modern pieces of many types – especially in Chapter 19, The Orchestra, and Chapter 27, Experimental Music.

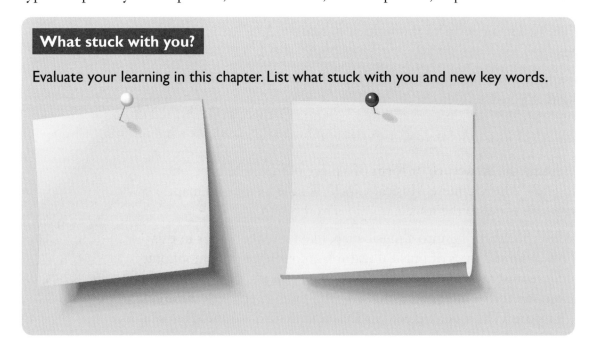

What stuck with you?

Evaluate your learning in this chapter. List what stuck with you and new key words.

Comparing Different Pieces of Music

Our new understanding of the **elements of music** allows us to listen more perceptively to the music we have heard in this unit. We must also be able to compare and contrast different pieces of music. This may seem difficult at first, but as our listening skills improve we will find it less daunting.

Listen to the following pieces:

'Golliwogg's Cakewalk' from *Children's Corner* by Debussy

Piano Concerto No. 2 in C minor (first movement excerpt) by Rachmaninov

Debussy with his daughter Chou-Chou, for whom *Children's Corner* was written

Rachmaninov's piece was written in 1900 but stylistically belongs very much to the Romantic era. Debussy's piece was written only a few years later, in 1908, but in a more modern style.

Find out when each composer was born, and work out how old they were when they were writing these pieces. Then listen again, and **compare and contrast the two performances** using the Venn diagram below to report your findings.

Rachmaninov

Golliwogg's Cakewalk   **Piano Concerto No. 2**

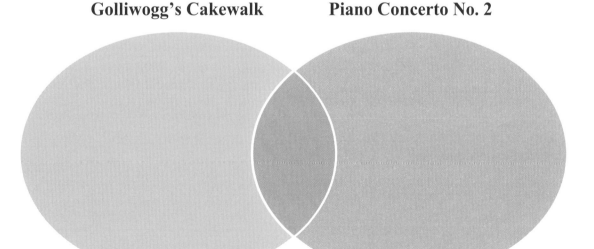

Choose and listen to a piece of music composed by Irish composers John Field, Brian Boydel and Ina Boyle. Choose two and use a Venn diagram to compare and contrast them.

Writing a programme note

Choose one of these pieces and complete some research on it. Write a programme note, including the following points:

A brief introduction to the composer
The circumstances surrounding the composition, and why the composer chose to write this music
What was happening in the composer's country at the time of the composition
The voices or instruments involved
Interesting musical points to listen out for
Your favourite section of the piece, and why

How the musical elements are used

Choose three elements of music from those we have studied. Then choose one of the pieces we have studied in this unit or another piece you know well, and report the role of each element in this work in the grid below. Refer to the music in your answer.

Musical element	Description
	Piece: Composer:
	Piece: Composer:
	Piece: Composer:

Music history timeline – revision

In this unit we have experienced lots of wonderful music, representing the artistic creativity of composers across a long period of history.

Each of the composers we have listened to belonged to one of the main eras of music history. On the timeline below, write in the names of the eras we have learned about: Baroque, Classical, Romantic and Modern. Then add the composers to their place in time, and use your research skills to identify another composer from the same period but from a different country. We will look at more composers from the modern era in the next two units.

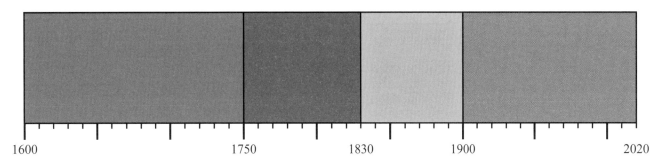

1600	1750	1830	1900 2020

One important thing to bear in mind: the change of style from one era to another was never sudden. There was a lot of overlap. Rachmaninov and Debussy, whom you compared earlier, are perfect examples. Rachmaninov lived till 1943 but was always a Romantic composer; his music is often described as 'late Romantic'. Debussy was older, but his music was always forward-looking, full of modern ideas.

What stuck with you?

Evaluate your learning in this chapter. List what stuck with you and new key words.

Reflection and Evaluation Sheet

Unit title:

Music I listened to:

Learning

Learning and exploring

I really enjoyed…

Something interesting I learned…

I excelled at…

My biggest challenge was…

I overcame this by…

I would like to learn more about…

New key words

Skills I developed in this unit…

This unit reminded me of learning about…

Goal setting…

-
-
-

Rate your learning

The Conducting Lab

In this unit

In this unit you will explore the role of conductors and determine the skills required for communicating music to musicians. Conducting pieces of music will provide you with an opportunity to actively participate in your learning and demonstrate your understanding of pulse and meter. Through study of orchestral instruments you will build on your knowledge of the orchestra. Listening and appraising pieces of orchestral music will develop your awareness of the complex decisions made by composers during the creative process. This knowledge will inspire your own creativity, helping you to appreciate the importance of experimenting and improvising. You will investigate how contemporary composers use found sounds and graphic scores to communicate their ideas. You will participate in activities which allow you to communicate your own creative ideas to others.

Intended learning

Create and present a short piece, using instruments and/or other sounds in response to a stimulus.

Read, interpret and play from symbolic representations of sounds.

Perform music at sight through clapping rhythmic phrases.

Demonstrate an understanding of a range of metres and pulses through conducting.

Experiment and improvise with making different types of sounds on a sound source and notate a brief piece that incorporates the sounds by devising symbolic representations for these sounds.

1.2,
1.5, 1.7,
1.9
2.1, 2.5, 2.9
3.3, 3.10,
3.11

Prepare and rehearse conducting a musical work for an ensemble focusing on cooperation and listening for balance.

Distinguish between the sonorities, ranges and timbres of selections of orchestral instruments; identify how these sounds are produced and propose their strengths and limitations in performance.

Make a study of a particular contemporary or musical style; analyse its structures and use of musical devices.

Discuss the principles of music property rights and explain how this can impact on the sharing and publishing of music.

Explore the time allocated to Irish conductors in local or national Irish media.

What Do Conductors Do?

A **conductor** is one of the most recognised roles in the orchestra, but what do you think a conductor actually does?

Role of the Conductor

We can trace the role of the conductor back to Ancient Greece. A document from 709BCE describes Pherekydes of Patrae, which means 'Giver of Rhythm', sitting up high, leading a group of 800 musicians by beating a golden staff so that the musicians played at the same time and kept together.

Andrew Davis conducting the Last Night of the Proms

Ensembles

In the last chapter we listened to various performances from different musical eras. Each performance had its own unique combination of players, using various groupings of instruments.

Groups of musicians who come together in this way are called **ensembles**. Some types of music ensemble are identified by distinct names such as **orchestra**, **quartet**, **trio** or **consort**. Some ensembles consist solely of instruments; others involve vocalists too.

We previously read about music ensembles in our community; can you name two?

_____

_____

 Research these ensemble formats and record your findings in the table below. List one well-known group for each category.

Ensemble	Description
String quartet	
Chamber choir	
Consort	
Marching band	

When a large group of musicians come together to play a piece of music it can be challenging to perform the music accurately. Many issues arise around tempo, dynamics, and an individual performer's interpretation of the music. For this reason, large ensembles always have a **conductor**.

Band of the Royal Irish Regiment

The Conductor's Role

The conductor's role has gradually developed, but above all it is about **communication**. Conductors are masters of communication as they rely on gestures rather than speech – hand, arm and facial signals – to communicate with musicians in an ensemble.

Other important skills for conductors include:

◆ **Research and planning**
Conductors must be familiar with the musical eras and styles. In order to communicate how the piece should be performed, a conductor must be able to interpret the tempo markings, mood and style of the music. In early music, composers didn't include tempo markings on their scores, so a conductor needs to choose the tempo based on their knowledge and judgement. The orchestra's seating plan is also decided by the conductor. This can vary depending on the venue, the era or style of the music being performed and other aspects such as whether or not there are soloists involved.

◆ **Concentration**
A conductor is always multi-tasking! They must bring the musical score to life! He or she must be able to read and understand the entire **score** at speed, while coordinating the musicians, **tempo**, **dynamics** and all other elements of the performance.

◆ **Listening**
Conductors must quickly recognise **pitch** inaccuracies or issues with tuning. They need expert knowledge of the capabilities of each instrument: **timbre**, **range** and tuning.

◆ **Clarity**
Conductors must ensure their gestures are consistent and that the directions they give are clearly defined and understood by all.

◆ **Cooperation**
They must establish a good relationship with members of the ensemble, with mutual trust. A performing ensemble is an excellent example of teamwork, cooperation and friendship!

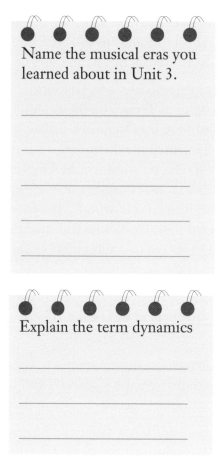

Name the musical eras you learned about in Unit 3.

_____

_____

_____

_____

Explain the term dynamics

_____

_____

_____

Range

The **range** of an instrument describes how high and how low it can play, particularly the highest and lowest notes.

75

Eímear Noone

Eímear Noone is an Irish video-game **composer** and **conductor**. Now resident in California, she grew up in East Galway. As a little girl, she was inspired by a white-haired gentleman in a tuxedo conducting an orchestra from a podium! From that moment she believed she would do the same. Overcoming stereotypes, with no real role-models to follow, Eímear set off on a rewarding adventure full of ups and downs, but ultimately success!

Before relocating to California, Eímear completed her studies at Trinity College, Dublin, and co-founded the Dublin City Orchestra. Today she is a successful and established conductor who has worked with many distinguished orchestras. In recent years she co-founded the Dublin International Game Music Festival. Her composing work includes music for *World of Warcraft*, and her piece 'Warlords of Draenor' received a Hollywood 'Music in the Media' award in 2014 for Best Video Game Score. Nintendo filmed Eímear conducting a symphony orchestra to create the first 3D footage of a symphony orchestra for the Nintendo 3DS.

Aged 12, Eímear wrote in a career guidance class 'When I grow up I want to conduct orchestras in Vienna'. She became the first woman to conduct in the National Concert Hall in Dublin. There are still few women conductors, though the number is increasing all the time.

Eímear was driven by her passion for music and what it stirred up in her. From a young age, she visualised and believed in her ability to become a composer and conductor. She was resilient, driven and diligent in realising this dream.

There are many videos of Eímear conducting her music online. Search online for a five-minute video entitled 'IMRO Interview with leading film/TV/Games composer and conductor Eímear Noone'. This provides insights into the work of a conductor of video-game music.

Discuss:

◆ Why do you think so few women have become conductors?

◆ What other careers in music do you feel might not be taken up by women, and why?

◆ What career or role are you passionate about?

◆ Do we need to be passionate about our future jobs? Why?

◆ Name two other Irish conductors.

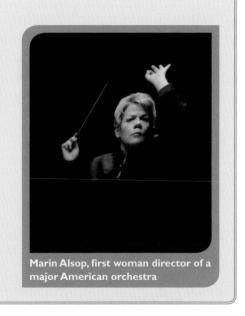

Marin Alsop, first woman director of a major American orchestra

Leonard Bernstein

Leonard Bernstein rose to prominence as music director of the New York Philharmonic Orchestra, known for his flamboyant conducting style and for his inspiring television talks on music. He was also a composer, specially known for his score to the musical *West Side Story*.

Do some research into *West Side Story* and answer this question.

On which Shakespeare play is *West Side Story* based, and in what way?

_____

_____

_____

Research any famous conductors and write some notes about what was special about them and what they achieved. Some possible names would be: Simon Rattle, Henry Wood, Odaline de la Martinez.

_____

_____

_____

_____

_____

_____

_____

What stuck with you?

Evaluate your learning in this chapter. List what stuck with you and new key words.

How to Conduct

Get started

Conductors use a **baton**, held in their right hand. It works by magnifying the conductor's gestures, helping musicians to understand what is being communicated to them.

Conductors take great care with their posture and actions. Every movement they make communicates information to the musicians who are following their lead.

Let's try it!

Stance Stand confidently with feet apart, one slightly in front of the other. Keep your head upright and avoid tapping your foot: this is distracting for your musicians and your audience.

Arms Place your arms out in front of you, parallel to the floor, elbows bent and away from your body to give you free space to move. In this ready position, your hands should be slightly above your wrists. Hold your baton in your right hand, while your left palm faces the floor with fingers slightly bent.

Your hands should not imitate each other. Right and left hands have a specific and important job: **the right to beat time** and the **left to communicate the expressive elements** of the music, such as dynamics.

Conductors create their gestures within a set space known as a **conductor's plane**. Imagine you have a **horizontal** line in front of you. You indicate the beat by tapping onto this horizontal line using your right-hand movements. The up movement before you begin prepares musicians for the first beat of the bar, the **downbeat**.

Your left hand uses a separate **vertical** space along the left hand side of your body, from your waist to the top of your head. Within this space, conductors communicate information such as dynamics or prepare performers for their entry.

British conductor Daniel Harding in rehearsal

Search online for 'Nintendo World Report recording of The Legend of Zelda on its 25th anniversary'. The conductor is Eímear Noone.

When you have found it, watch the video, and answer the following questions:

1 Do you recognise any instruments used in this ensemble?

2 Which hand holds the baton? _____

3 Which musical features are controlled by the left hand?

4 Are the musicians watching her? _____

5 What other communications does she make with the musicians?

6 Does she have a good rapport with them? Give reasons for your answer.

YouTube is a huge resource which allows you to watch professional conductors at work and study how they convey their wishes to the performers.

Time Signatures

Conducting is communication through gesture and takes a lot of work to perfect. With a continuous pattern they show the beat or pulse, while reading the music in front of them.

So what's on that page that's so important? The written music is divided on the **stave** by vertical lines known as **barlines**. Each barline organises the pulse or beats into **measures** or **bars**, which are controlled by a **time signature**. The conductor's right hand pattern indicates the time signature of the music being performed.

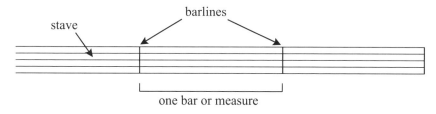

The **time signature** indicates how many beats or pulses there are in each bar. A time signature consist of two numbers, one on top of the other, placed at the beginning of a piece of music.

Both numbers indicate important information.

◆ The top number states how many beats there are in each bar.

◆ The bottom number tells us the duration or time-value of each beat.

For the next activity, we are interested in the top number. This tells us how many beats we must indicate in our conducting pattern.

Conducting Patterns

There are three basic patterns for conductors to master: the Two, Three and Four patterns.

Before we begin, remember:

◆ The importance of the **upbeat**. It's a preparatory 'get ready' for musicians to know when a new bar is about to begin.

◆ The horizontal line. This is an imaginary line but an important guide for the musicians taking your lead.

Here are the three patterns:

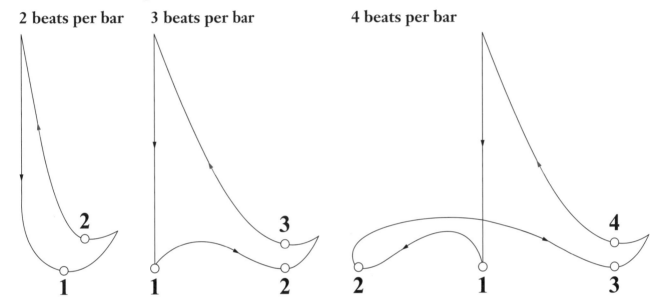

A great way to begin learning these patterns is to trace them with your finger, then try them out in the air. Once you are confident you know the patterns, stand up and demonstrate them. Remember the important points we learned earlier about a conductor's stance and arm position. Use a pencil or chopstick to simulate a baton and you will really look the part!

The most common time signatures are:

$$\frac{2}{4}, \frac{3}{4} \text{ and } \frac{4}{4}.$$

The Two, Three and Four conducting patterns are used to conduct pieces of music in these time signatures. Examine the grid below; each time signature is shown with its way of counting the pulse. Counting the **pulse** aloud will help you understand these time signatures. Whilst counting, emphasise the number **1**s – this is the first beat of each bar.

$\frac{2}{4}$	2 beats per bar	1 2 1 2 1 2 1 2 1 2 1 2
$\frac{3}{4}$	3 beats per bar	1 2 3 1 2 3 1 2 3 1 2 3
$\frac{4}{4}$	4 beats per bar	1 2 3 4 1 2 3 4 1 2 3 4 1 2 3 4

Practising conducting

Are you ready to conduct some music? The following examples will help you to test out your new patterns. Not all of these pieces of music are performed by ensembles, but you will enjoy conducting your patterns together.

Listen first and identify the **pulse**. You will notice that some sounds are emphasised. These are the first beat in each bar – and where you should begin the conducting pattern again if you get lost!

Listen and practise conducting these pieces of music.

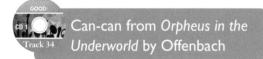

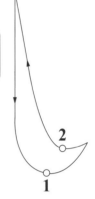

Other examples to try:

'I Love Rock 'n Roll' by Joan Jett & The Blackhearts

'When the saints go marching in'

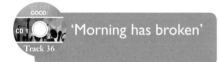

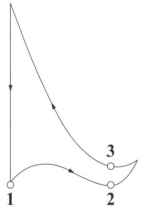

Other examples to try:

'The Times They Are a-Changing' by Bob Dylan

'How Can I be Sure' by Dusty Springfield

'Mull of Kintyre' by Wings

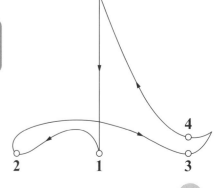

Other examples to try:

'Always Look on the Bright Side of Life' sung by Eric Idle

'I Will Survive' by Gloria Gaynor

'Tears of a Clown' by Smokey Robinson and the Miracles

Research and conduct

Choose a piece of music performed by an **ensemble** that you enjoy listening to. Do some research on this music and write a programme note for it.

 Present your **programme note** to your class. Play an excerpt from the music and perform a suitable conducting pattern for it. Consider the **tempo** and **dynamics** of the piece. Show instructions for dynamics using your left hand where necessary.

Title:	Composer/Artist:	Time signature:
Programme note		**Illustrate pattern used:**

What stuck with you?

Evaluate your learning in this chapter. List what stuck with you and new key words.

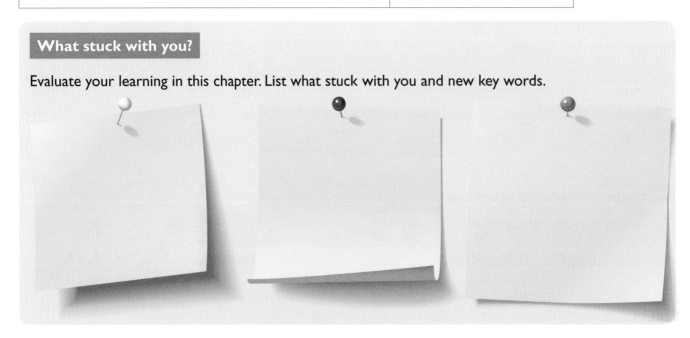

The **orchestra** is a large **ensemble** of musicians including four main families of instruments:

◆ Woodwind

◆ Strings

◆ Brass

◆ Percussion

Instruments belonging to each family are typically made of the same materials, look similar, and produce broadly the same **timbres** or sounds. Within each family some are larger than others. How will this affect the **pitch** of these instruments?

Examine the diagram below, which shows a typical seating plan for an orchestra.

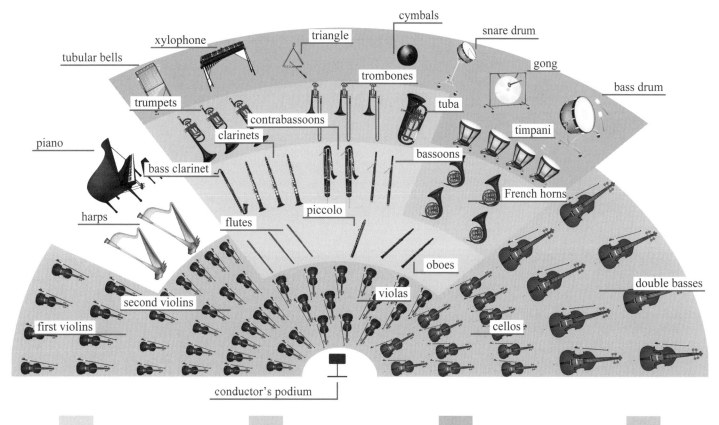

woodwind family   brass family   percussion instruments   violin family

The families of the orchestra are colour-coded above so we can see their location in the orchestra. Over the next few pages we will examine the instruments belonging to each family in greater detail.

What do you notice about the seating plan? Have you any ideas as to why the instruments might be organised in this way?

The Families of Orchestral Instruments

 Analyse the diagram below and discuss together the similarities and differences which exist between the instruments within each family.

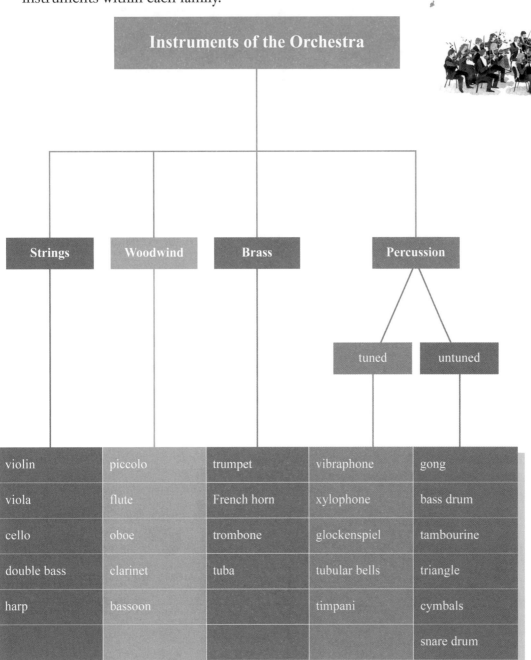

Instruments of the Orchestra

Strings	Woodwind	Brass	Percussion	
			tuned	untuned
violin	piccolo	trumpet	vibraphone	gong
viola	flute	French horn	xylophone	bass drum
cello	oboe	trombone	glockenspiel	tambourine
double bass	clarinet	tuba	tubular bells	triangle
harp	bassoon		timpani	cymbals
				snare drum

Each instrument has its own capabilities and limitations. What does this mean? For example, one instrument's timbre may make it the perfect choice for a particular mood, but its **range** may limit the instrument's ability to perform the written melody.

Listen to the opening section of *The Young Person's Guide to the Orchestra* by Benjamin Britten. You should notice how the music moves from one family of instruments to another.

For more on this piece of music see page 89.

'Theme' from *The Young Person's Guide to the Orchestra* by Britten

Woodwind

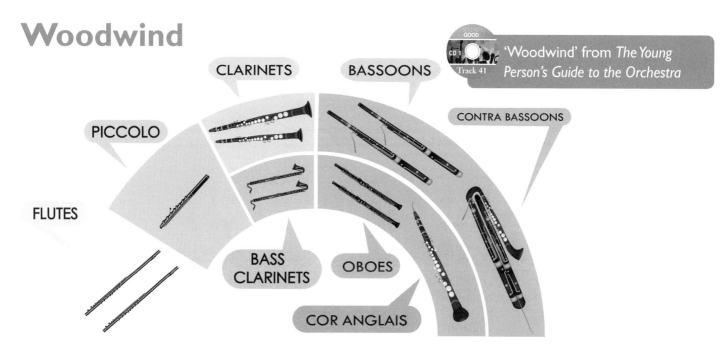

'Woodwind' from *The Young Person's Guide to the Orchestra*

CLARINETS

BASSOONS

CONTRA BASSOONS

PICCOLO

FLUTES

BASS CLARINETS

OBOES

COR ANGLAIS

Woodwind instruments add warmth to the orchestra and are seated behind the string family. As their name suggests, woodwind instruments are mainly made from wood, though nowadays they carry a lot of complicated metal keywork, and modern flutes are usually made of metal. Many types of woodwind instruments are used in the orchestra today, but most common are piccolo, flute, oboe, clarinet and bassoon.

Sound is produced by blowing air through the instrument, setting up vibrations. This is done either by blowing across a hole in the mouthpiece (for piccolos and flutes) or blowing through a **reed** (most other woodwind instruments). The reed is attached to the mouthpiece and is usually made of bamboo cane.

Work on your own to research these woodwind instruments. Identify the range of each instrument and consider its capabilities and limitations. Record your findings in the table below.

Instrument	Description and information	Well-known player
Piccolo		
Flute		
Oboe		
Clarinet		
Bassoon		

Strings

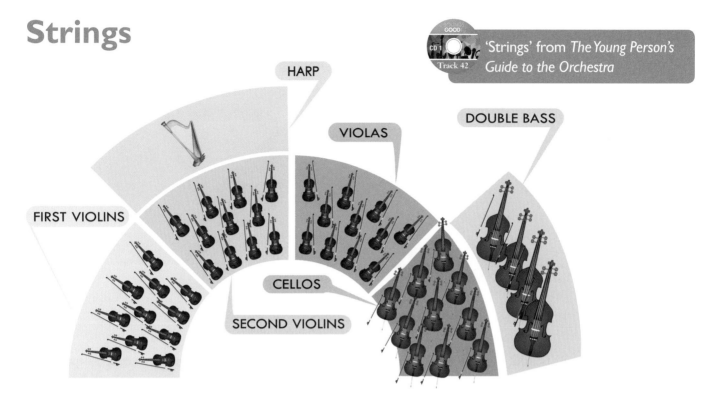

'Strings' from *The Young Person's Guide to the Orchestra*

The family of **string** instruments consists of four bowed instruments – violin, viola, cello and double bass, and one plucked instrument – the harp. Numerically it is the largest family in the orchestra and is seated at the front.

Each of the bowed instruments in the family has four strings, stretched across a hollow wooden body, which amplifies the vibrations made when a bow is drawn across the strings.

The **bow** used to play the violin has a shaped wooden part which holds a tightly stretched bundle of horsehair strands, which are drawn across the violin strings causing them to vibrate. Sometimes the bow is not used and musicians **pluck** the strings with their fingers. This performing technique is called **pizzicato**. Some composers have written other directions such as **col legno**, which asks the player to play with the wooden stick on the strings, creating an interesting percussive sound.

 Work in pairs to research these instruments. Identify the range of each instrument and consider its capabilities and limitations. Record your findings in the table below.

Instrument	Description and information	Well-known player
Violin		
Viola		
Cello		
Double bass		
Harp		

Brass

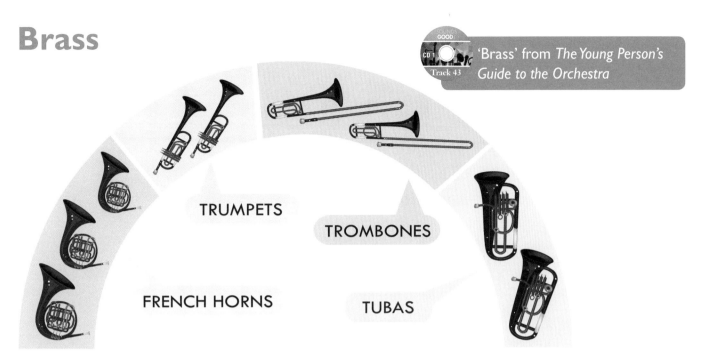

'Brass' from *The Young Person's Guide to the Orchestra*

TRUMPETS

TROMBONES

FRENCH HORNS

TUBAS

Brass instruments trumpets, french horns, trombones and tubas essentially consist of a metal tube with a mouthpiece at one end and a flared bell-shaped opening at the other. As performers blow, they use their lips to create vibrations in the instrument. The tube is shaped and coiled into various forms for the different instruments. The length of open tube can be varied either by a slide (for trombones) or by finger-operated valves (most other brass instruments), thereby producing different notes.

Brass instruments are recognised by their majestic sound and are often used to play thrilling, dramatic music like **fanfares**. They are louder than the strings and woodwind, so they are seated towards the back of the orchestra. Performers sometimes use **mutes**, placed into the open end of the instrument to dampen or vary the sound. 'Con sordino' is often written on scores. This means 'with mute'.

Work together to research each of these brass instruments. Identify the range of each instrument and consider its capabilities and limitations. Record your findings in the table below.

Instrument	Description and information	Well-known player
Trumpet		
French horn		
Trombone		
Tuba		

Percussion

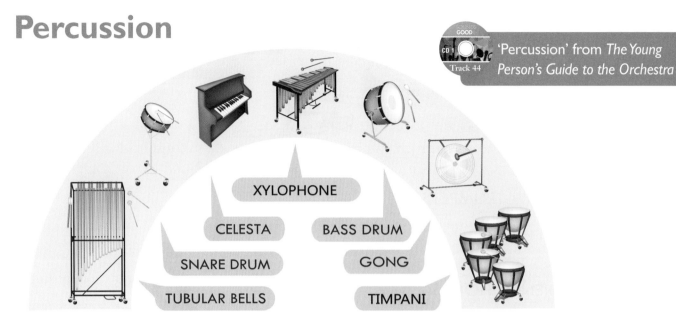

CD 1 Track 44 'Percussion' from *The Young Person's Guide to the Orchestra*

Bang, clash, boom! The **percussion** family is the loudest family of all, and they are seated at the back of the orchestra. There are two main types: **pitched** and **unpitched** (or non-pitched).

- Pitched percussion instruments, as their name implies, can play different pitches or notes, including melodies if required. Xylophone, timpani and tubular bells are examples.

- Unpitched instruments produce sounds of indefinite pitch. They play rhythm patterns and various sound effects. Bass drum, cymbals and triangle are examples.

 Work in pairs to research each of the percussion instruments below. Identify the range of each, and consider its capabilities and limitations. Record your findings in the table below.

Instrument	Description and information	Pitched or unpitched
Timpani		
Tubular bells		
Bass drum		
Cymbals		
Xylophone		
Gong		
Snare drum		

Composing for Orchestra

Composers have so much choice! How do they choose what instruments should play their compositions? The size of an orchestra can range from 25 to 100 musicians. What considerations do you think **composers** might make when choosing an instrument or family of instruments for their music?

Benjamin Britten 1913–1976
Composer and pianist

The Young Person's Guide to the Orchestra

Britten's celebrated work *The Young Person's Guide to the Orchestra* is based on a melody by Henry Purcell, a prolific Baroque composer who has been an important influence on many modern composers.

Purcell's melody was part of the music he composed in 1695 to accompany a play called *Abdelazar*. Britten took the melody and used it to compose his orchestral masterpiece, written in 1946 for a documentary film designed to demonstrate the instruments of the orchestra, their sound and capabilities.

First we are introduced to the melody by the full orchestra, followed by each of the families so that it soon becomes familiar. Then he presents a set of variations featuring each instrument in turn, in order of family and pitch, highest to lowest. Britten ends the piece with a scurrying **fugue**, leading to a final grand statement of the theme.

 'Fugue' from *The Young Person's Guide to the Orchestra* by Britten

Try making a **music map** which charts the different sections of the piece. Note which family or instrument is featured in each section, and pay attention to the dynamic variations. This is a long work, so you may need to listen to the individual sections to help you identify the instruments.

List the instruments in the grid below as you hear them. Categorise them according to the family they belong to.

Fugue

A fugue is a piece of music in which a short melody or phrase is introduced by one part and successively taken up by others and developed by interweaving the parts.

Variations

Many composers have written sets of variations, taking a theme and presenting it in many different ways.

Try singing the melody of 'Twinkle twinkle little star', then repeating the first phrase in as many different ways as you can find. What changes can you make?

Woodwind	Strings	Brass	Percussion

More music for orchestra

 YouTube is a great resource for listening to classical music, and indeed to music of all sorts. To experience how composers have written for the orchestra, try listening to and analysing the following pieces:

- *Finlandia* by Sibelius
- *Mother Goose Suite* by Ravel
- *Bolero* by Ravel
- *Four Sea Interludes* by Britten
- *Prélude a l'apres midi d'un faun* by Debussy
- Overture to *The Marriage of Figaro* by Mozart

- Symphony No. 6 (Pastoral) by Beethoven
- 'Galop' from *The Comedians* by Kabalevsky
- 'Sabre Danse' by Khachaturian
- 'The Hut on Fowl's Legs' from *Pictures at an Exhibition* by Mussorgsky

Then choose one of them, investigate the composer, and write a review for a music magazine. You should include information about:

- The composer
- The style and historical era the work belongs to
- The orchestration

- Other interesting details such as tempo, mood and dynamics
- Interesting musical points to listed out for

Title of your chosen piece: _____

Your review: _____

_____

_____

_____

What stuck with you?

Evaluate your learning in this chapter. List what stuck with you and new key words.

Conductors must be able to read music, especially rhythms, as they are required to beat time! In this chapter and the next, we will look at notation, scores, notes and note-values, and a bit more about time signatures.

Music Scores

Look at this image, taken from a musical manuscript. Consider what this image is communicating to you.

We know it is 'music', but do we understand how and why it is being communicated in this way? Writing it down establishes the existence of a piece of music and protects it from being lost or forgotten. It communicates the composer's intentions to performers. Musicians perform music by interpreting the symbols composers write.

In earlier chapters, we listened to **ensembles** performing marvellous music and discussed the conductor's role in communicating music to performers. The conductor has a **score**, and the players have their own **parts**. It may look tricky, but for them reading sheet music is a bit like reading information on a map. The symbols on the page are so familiar that they can navigate and interpret the information very quickly. By the end of this unit you will too!

The Stave

Let's begin with a blank map and add information to it as we go.

Our starting point is called the **stave**. It consists of five horizontal **lines**, with four **spaces** in between. Take a moment to count these on the stave below.

We read a stave both horizontally (indicating time) and vertically (indicating pitch), rather like the way we read the coordinates on a map or a graph.

Treble clef

This is a **treble clef**, also known as a **G clef**:

This is how it is written on the stave:

Guido used a clef on each stave, and we still follow this practice. The clef is a symbol which signifies where a particular **pitch** can be found on the stave.

I'm sure you have seen the treble clef before. Try drawing one. Look carefully at the one above to help you while you practise drawing it on the stave below.

Coordinates

You will have learned in your geography lessons that maps include horizontal and vertical lines marking latitude and longitude. These can be used to give the **coordinates** or exact location of a place. In science or maths, coordinates identify points on a graph.

What are the coordinates of your school? Discuss different ways coordinates are used in maps or in graphs.

Guido of Arezzo

Guido was an eleventh-century monk who revolutionised music by inventing the stave. He developed a system that used four lines and a **clef** to help musicians to identify a sound or pitch to begin with. In time, a fifth line was added, giving us our stave as we recognise it today.

Guido of Arezzo

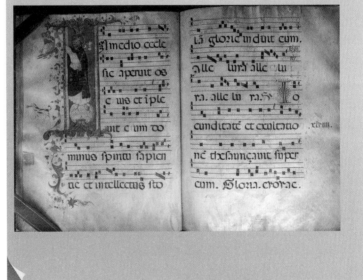

Double barline

This is a double barline. It is used to indicate the end of a piece of music. Notice that the second line is thicker than the first.

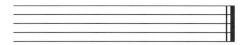

Use a ruler to draw a stave in the box below. Lines should be evenly spaced and parallel. Draw a treble clef at the beginning of the stave and a double barline at the end.

Parallel lines

What have you learned about parallel lines?

Two parallel lines must lie in the same plane. They are always the same distance apart; they do not intersect.

Do you know how to draw parallel lines using a ruler and set square?

Rhythm and beat are not the same

All music has rhythm. So what exactly is it?

Rhythm is the arrangement of sounds in time.

We write rhythms using symbols that indicate the relative length or time value of the notes we place on the stave.

Remember, rhythm is not the same as 'beat' or 'pulse'. Beat is a constant steady pulse in music, just like the beat of your heart. **Rhythm is the more complex patterns heard within the beats**.

Listen to songs with a distinctive rhythm pattern. For instance:

◆ 'Perfect' by Ed Sheeran

◆ 'When the saints go marching in'

◆ 'We Will Rock You' by Queen

Split the class in half.

◆ Group 1: Tap the **pulse** of the song with your foot.

◆ Group 2: Clap the **rhythm** pattern of the melody.

When we identify the pulse or beat of a piece of music, we notice that some beats are more pronounced or emphasised than others. This tells us how the beats are organised within the bars, marked by the barlines on the stave.

Rhythms are easily recognised in a piece of music. So what do they look like on the stave?

Composers use symbols to represent the **note values** or duration of sounds. Each note value has its own symbol so we can tell them apart. Let's take a look.

Note Values

A **crotchet**, also known as a **quarter note** is drawn as an oval-shaped notehead with a stem. The notehead is filled in completely. Crotchets are often, *but not always*, equal to 1 beat or pulse.

A **minim**, also known as a **half note**, is equal to 2 crotchets. It is drawn as an oval-shaped notehead with a stem, but unlike the crotchet its notehead is never filled in.

A **semibreve**, also known as a **whole note**, is equal to 4 crotchets. It is drawn on the stave as an oval-shaped notehead and has no stem. Its notehead is never filled in.

A **quaver**, also known as an **eighth note**, is a little trickier to draw. It is equal to half a crotchet. For this reason there are often two quavers together. A single quaver starts off looking like a crotchet, but with a **tail**, also known as a **flag**, added to the stem.

When **two quavers** are written together, we join them with a **beam** in place of the two individual tails. Three or more quavers can be joined by a beam in the same way.

Study this diagram, showing the note values in a pyramid. It will help you to understand the note values in relation to each other.

How to write the notes

Let's take some time to practise drawing these symbols.

Look closely at them before you begin. The notehead and stems are important details. Noteheads are oval in shape and stems must be straight. Draw the stems up from the *right-hand edge of the notehead*, not the centre. (Stems can also go down, in which case they go down from the *left-hand* edge of the notehead, but we will learn more about that later.)

Aim for consistency in your work; each crotchet should look the same.

Copy this exercise onto the blank stave below.

Dotted notes

You may see notes in a piece of music with a dot to the right of the notehead. These are called **dotted notes**. The dot increases the time-value of the note by an additional half of its original value, making it one-and-a-half times as long.

Compare the note values below to their dotted equivalent.

Note	Value in crotchets	Note	Value in crotchets
𝅝	4 crotchets	𝅝·	6 crotchets
𝅗𝅥	2 crotchets	𝅗𝅥·	3 crotchets
𝅘𝅥	1 crotchet	𝅘𝅥·	one-and-a-half crotchets
𝅘𝅥𝅮	half a crotchet	𝅘𝅥𝅮·	three-quarters of a crotchet

Musical maths

Complete these musical sums. The first one is done for you.

𝅘𝅥 + 𝅘𝅥 = 𝅗𝅥

𝅘𝅥 + 𝅘𝅥𝅮𝅘𝅥𝅮 = ___

𝅘𝅥 + 𝅘𝅥𝅮 = ___

𝅝 + 𝅗𝅥 = ___

𝅗𝅥 + 𝅘𝅥𝅮𝅘𝅥𝅮 + 𝅘𝅥𝅮𝅘𝅥𝅮 = ___

𝅗𝅥· + 𝅗𝅥· = ___

𝅗𝅥· + 𝅗𝅥· + 𝅘𝅥 = ___

𝅗𝅥 + 𝅗𝅥· + 𝅘𝅥𝅮 = ___

What stuck with you?

Evaluate your learning in this chapter. List what stuck with you and new key words.

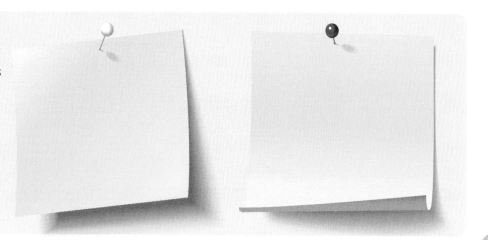

The Rhythm of Words

Let's start with our own names. Each of us has a rhythm pattern in our name.

Write your first name here: _____

How many **syllables** does it have? This tells you how many rhythm notes to give it. Are the syllables long or short sounds? Maybe they are equal? Create a rhythm pattern for it above the syllables.

Here are some examples to consider – but they have become mixed up. Draw lines to match the correct rhythm pattern to each name.

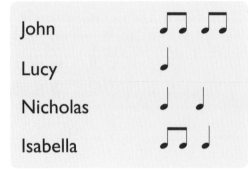

Songwriters like to match suitable rhythm patterns to their lyrics. Most of the time, each **syllable** gets one note, though sometimes a syllable can be stretched over several notes.

Sort the words below to their matching rhythm pattern.

Phoenix Park

River Liffey

Four Courts

Dublin Castle

George's Dock

Croke Park

Lamb Alley

Pearse Station

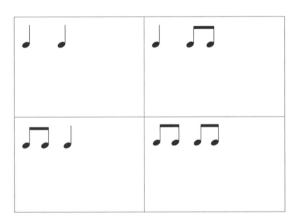

Time Signatures

We have explored how conductors use gestures to guide musicians in ensembles. Each conducting pattern indicates a particular **time signature**, with the first beat of each bar shown by the downbeat. Look back at Chapter 18 to remind yourself about this.

List the three time signatures we worked with.

Remember, the top number of a time signature tells us how many beats or pulses there are in each bar and in its corresponding conducting pattern.

Time signatures are added to our musical map next to the clef, like this:

Composers organise their rhythm patterns within the time signature using barlines. **Time signatures** tell us the number of beats and the type of notes that each bar contains. The top number is the number of beats per bar; the bottom number tells us what type of note is used for the beat.

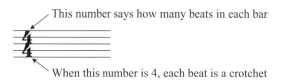

This number says how many beats in each bar

When this number is 4, each beat is a crotchet

If the bottom number is 4, that means the beat is a crotchet. (Remember, the other name for crotchet is 'quarter note'.) The most common time signatures have 4 as the bottom number.

Here are some examples of time signatures in action. Remember to look at the top number: it tells you how many beats there are in each bar.

Count and clap together. Place more emphasis on the first beat of each bar.

These examples only use crotchets, so they are not very interesting musically. In fact, they aren't really rhythm patterns, they are just the basic pulse.

Rhythm patterns

The three examples on the previous page only use one pitch, so they don't really need a clef and stave; we can write them on a rhythm line. Now look at three more examples, using the same time signatures but with more interesting rhythms.

Count and clap together.

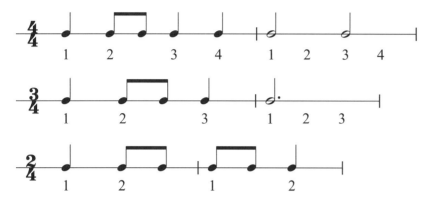

Examine how the beats move steadily onwards, whatever the note values.

Investigate the rhythms below. Consider the time signature, and insert barlines where they should be. Each rhythm starts on the first beat of the bar. Finish by adding a double barline.

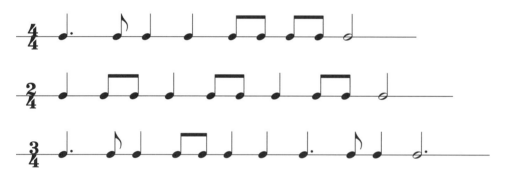

Clap the rhythms, remembering to emphasise the first beat in every bar.

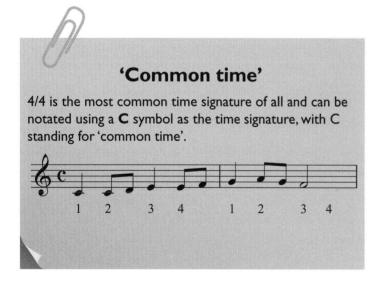

'Common time'

4/4 is the most common time signature of all and can be notated using a **C** symbol as the time signature, with C standing for 'common time'.

Changing time signatures are a feature of many twentieth-century compositions. Irish composer Gerald Barry makes over 330 time signature changes in his Piano Quartet No.1!

The sound of silence

What is silence? Have you ever considered the role of silence in a piece of music?

Music contains both sound and silence. There are symbols, called **rests**, that can be used to notate periods of silence in a piece of music. They are used in the score, just like notes. Each note value has an equivalent rest, as follows:

Clap this very common bass drum rhythm, and indicate the correct time signature at the beginning.

Here are three more rhythms for you to identify the time signature.

Now look at this tune, apply the missing barlines. It starts on the first beat of the bar.

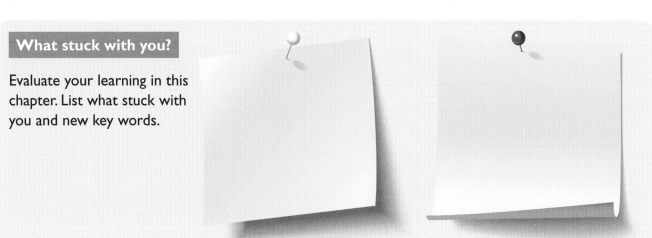

What stuck with you?

Evaluate your learning in this chapter. List what stuck with you and new key words.

Reflection and Evaluation Sheet

Unit title:

Music I listened to:

Learning and exploring

I really enjoyed…

Something interesting I learned…

I excelled at…

My biggest challenge was…

I overcame this by…

I would like to learn more about…

New key words

Skills I developed in this unit…

This unit reminded me of learning about…

Goal setting…

-
-
-

Rate your learning

Composing Lab

In this unit

In this unit you will explore your creative talent in an imaginative and reflective way. You will explore how music is constructed and how sounds can be communicated to musicians in written format. You will learn how to use symbols to represent sound and create short musical motifs and soundscapes. You will bring musical ideas to life by experimenting with this new knowledge. You and your classmates will create and present your compositions, reflect on and evaluate your work. Skills you will develop in this unit include brainstorming, researching, practising, presenting, capturing, evaluating and reflecting. You will begin to gather and compile evidence of your creative compositional endeavours. Samples of your compositional efforts will be chosen for submission as part of your CBA1 Compositional Portfolio.

Intended learning

Design a rhythmic accompaniment and improvise over a recording.

Listen to and transcribe rhythmic phrases of up to two bars.

Create a musical statement and share with others the statement's purpose and development.

Illustrate the structure of a piece of music through a physical or visual representation.

1.2, 1.3, 1.6, 1.11 2.2, 2.4, 2.6, 2.7 3.4

Create and present some musical ideas using instruments and/or found sounds to illustrate moods or feelings.

Rehearse and present a song or brief instrumental piece; identify and reflect on the techniques that were necessary to interpret the music effectively.

Design a rhythmic ostinato and add a layer of sound over the pattern as it repeats.

Compose and perform an original jingle or brief piece of music for use in a new advertisement for a product, and record the composition.

The English composer Frederick Delius said 'There is only one real happiness in life, and that is the happiness of creativity'.

What does creativity mean?

_____

_____

Composers combine their **creativity** with compositional skills to construct music. Anyone can become a composer! Composing music is rewarding and fun.

In this unit we will explore the theory and techniques involved in creating a musical composition, combining this new knowledge with the elements of music which we studied in previous lessons.

Composers rarely create something from nothing. They are inspired and motivated by experiences of all sorts. They also need to apply their knowledge of music theory. Composing music is really about bringing together the many working parts of music: the sum is often greater than the parts.

Our goal is to create something new and unique. This unit will help you to develop your compositional skills.

Percussionist Tito Puente

Inventing rhythms

Now that you know how to notate rhythms, you can create some rhythms of your own – and write them down in notation.

Compose a rhythm part for performance on a percussion instrument.

Investigate the example below, and perform it. Notice that it is in 3/4 time, and emphasise the first beat of each bar.

Then compose your own rhythm – but in 4/4 – and indicate it on the rhythm line below. Clap the rhythms you create to test how well they work. You may decide to adapt your initial pattern and make some adjustments to it.

What instrument (or instruments) would you propose to play your rhythm?

Work with a classmate to compose four bars of 4/4 rhythm in two parts. Synthesise your ideas to compose a 2-part rhythm below. Rehearse and perform it for your classmates.

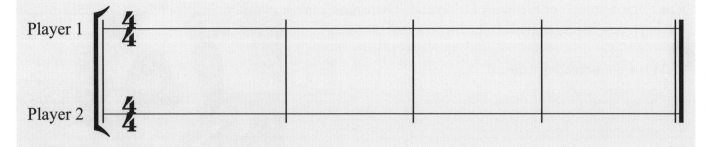

Matching words and rhythms

Compose and apply suitable lyrics to match the rhythm pattern below. Take care to write each syllable directly below its note.

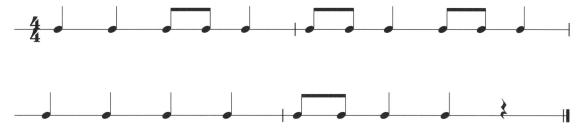

The Giraffe and the Pelly and me

Read this poem by Roald Dahl.

The Giraffe and the Pelly and me by Roald Dahl

> We will polish your glass
> Till it's shining like brass
> And it sparkles like sun on the sea!
> We will work for Your Grace
> Till we're blue in the face,
> The Giraffe and the Pelly and me!
>
> Roald Dahl

 What would be a suitable rhythm to go with these words? Working in pairs, experiment with speaking the words in a rhythmic way. As you begin to form an idea of the rhythm of the poem, identify the syllables, line by line, and assign a note value to each one.

Compose a rhythm pattern and indicate the words of the verse below the notes.

Include rests in your pattern if you wish, and don't forget to include the time signature, barlines and the final double barline.

As we're concentrating on rhythm here, you can use a single-line stave, like the ones at the top of the page.

 Rehearse and perform the poem with the rhythm you have worked out. You could do it in pairs. If you have recording facilities in your school, record it for your portfolio.

Does your performance match your written notation?

Improvisation

Improvisation is spontaneous creative activity. It requires us to compose in the moment. It is a fun way of reminding ourselves that music is instinctive and that we can play with it and experiment with it.

 Listen to this drum loop in 4/4 time. When you can comfortably identify the pulse, **improvise** by creating and performing rhythmic patterns over the track. To do this, clap any patterns you feel might fit. Feel loose, so that you enjoy doing it.

1 Did you enjoy this activity? If so, explain why.

_____

2 Define the term improvisation, in your own terms. What does it mean to you?

_____

_____

3 Could 'improvisation' be applied to any of the other arts or even to sport or other activities?

_____

_____

_____

4 What have you learned about rhythm?

_____

_____

Rhythm Exercises

Identifying rhythms

For each exercise, you will hear a rhythm. After listening to the pattern, identify the time signature and circle which rhythm pattern you heard.

 1a)  b)  c)

 2a)  b)  c)

Rhythm dictation exercises

 For each exercise, you will hear two bars of **rhythm** played three times. Identify the time signature and notate the rhythm pattern you hear in the bars below.

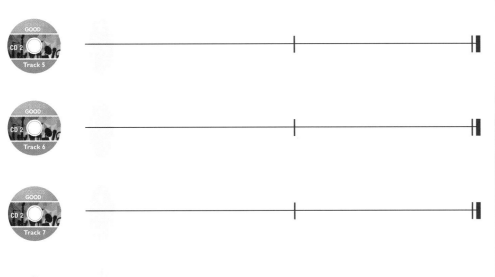

Dictation exercises are excellent practice for playing and listening as well as for notation, so ask your teacher to give you more exercises of this sort. You could even try devising them yourself and use them to test each other.

What stuck with you?

Evaluate your learning in this chapter. List what stuck with you and new key words.

Melody

To complete our musical map-making skills, we must learn how to apply pitches to our rhythm patterns. When **pitch** is added to **rhythm**, we produce **melody**.

Pitch + Rhythm = Melody

When we add a clef to the stave, we are identifying pitches. Each line or space on the stave represents a particular pitch.

The higher the note sits on a stave, the higher the pitch it represents.

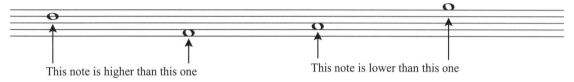

This note is higher than this one   This note is lower than this one

In the Western world we have been notating pitch for approximately a thousand years – which isn't very long in the grand scheme of things. Older traditions used symbols. Ancient Hindus and Greeks assigned letters, Persians used numbers, and the Chinese used other symbols. Western notation began to emerge from about 500AD. Monks developed the thinking of the Roman poet and philosopher Boethius, who used Latin letters to identify pitch.

Over time, the monks developed a system of placing marks called **neumes** over the text of their chants. Neumes represented the pitch, length of sounds and the movement from one note to the next. They later added a horizontal guide-line, with symbols drawn above or below the line: neumes above the line were higher in pitch than those below. This led to the work of Guido of Arezzo, who added more lines. Eventually we added the fifth line, and, hey presto, we have our stave!

The way music is notated continues to evolve today. We know this from our study of **graphic scores** – we will learn more about this in chapter 27 page 120.

Propose how music notation might change in the future.

Notes on the stave

The lines and spaces on the stave hold assigned pitches or sounds. Identify the semibreves on the stave below as being either on a **line** or in a **space**.

Draw a <u>triangle</u> around each note on a line, and a <u>square</u> around each note in a space.

Add numbers to the end of the stave to identify the five lines and four spaces, counting <u>upwards</u>.

Fixing the Pitch

Next, we add a treble clef, and that fixes the pitch for each line and space. Specifically, it fixes the second line up as G, and the other pitches follow from that.

To help us to learn the pitches we can start with this helpful **mnemonic**:

Every Good Boy Does Fine

A mnemonic is a memory-aid, for instance a phrase used to help us remember a sequence of letters.

Devise another mnemonic for the five lines below.

E_____ G_____ B_____

D_____ F_____

Draw a treble clef at the beginning of the stave below, and then identify the notes written on the stave, referring to the mnemonic until you remember all five lines and their notes.

In between the lines are four spaces. These are the four pitches named in those spaces (see right). They spell out the word FACE.

Draw a treble clef at the beginning of the stave below, and place the notes listed onto the stave as semibreves. In some cases you can choose between a line and a space, but be careful to choose the *right* line or space.

F   C   A   E   F   E   C   A

Let's put our new knowledge into practice. Name the notes below, writing the letter-name below each note.

The Musical Alphabet

Although there are five lines and four spaces, we have only used seven different letter-names:

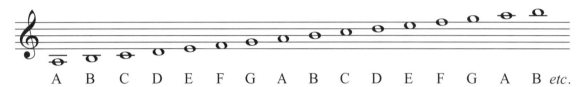

| A | B | C | D | E | F | and | G |

The top space and line have the same letter-names as the bottom line and space: E and F. This is because once we get to the note G, going up, we return to A and the pattern repeats, like this:

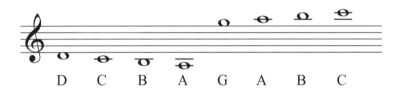

A B C D E F G A B C D E F G A B *etc*.

Ledger lines

More lines? You will notice that we have written more notes above and below the stave, using short extra lines. These are called **ledger lines**. They work as extensions of the stave, and notes are placed on the ledger lines or in the spaces between them, in just the same way as on the stave.

D C B A G A B C

Remembering that the top line is F, identify the notes in the exercise below:

....

The bottom line is E, identify the notes in the exercise below:

....

Drawing notation accurately

A semibreve is the easiest note to draw onto a stave. Its oval shape is easy to draw, but it is important to place it correctly on the chosen line or space. If on a line, the line should go right through the middle of the notehead. If in a space, the note should fill the space.

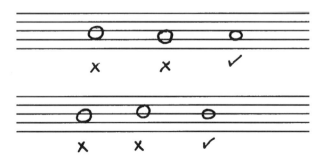

Stems

Minims, crotchets and quavers have **stems** attached to their noteheads. These should be straight and not too long or too short.

Stems can go up or down. Normally they go up when the notehead is in the lower half of the stave, and down if the notehead is in the upper half. Notes on the middle line normally have a down-stem. *Up-stems are written on the right hand side of the notehead, down-stems on the left hand side.* Look carefully at the examples shown to see this in action.

Notice that the quaver tails are always to the right of the stem, whether it's an up-stem or a down-stem.

Add stems to the noteheads below:

Most of the stems below are incorrectly drawn. Rewrite this short melody on the blank stave provided.

What stuck with you?

Evaluate your learning in this chapter. List what stuck with you and new key words.

Composing with Melody

Putting It Together

Demonstrate your new knowledge of pitch-writing with your rhythm-writing skills to compose a 4-bar melody in 4/4. Set out your 'map' – the treble clef and the 4/4 time signature – before you begin. Creating a rhythm pattern before adding pitch is good practice, so we have provided a rhythm line for sketching your rhythm patterns.

Sketch your rhythm patterns here:

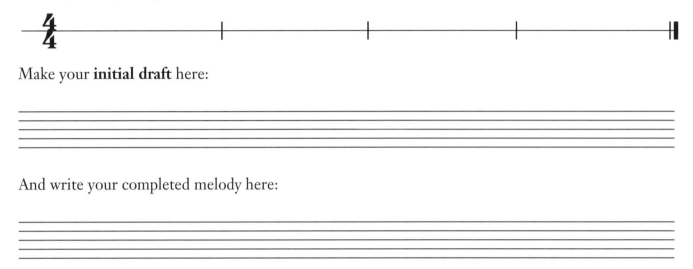

Make your **initial draft** here:

And write your completed melody here:

Hearing what you have created helps you to understand what makes a good melody.

◆ Clap the rhythm pattern you have chosen to see if you like it.

◆ Listen to your melody played on a piano by your teacher or a classmate.

◆ Or use software such as Score Creator, Finale Notepad or MuseScore to input your melody. Score Creator is designed for tablets or phones. With these programs, you will be able to play back your melody and appraise it.

Reflect on your melody, and make notes in the space below. How did it sound? Did it flow or jump? Was the rhythm busy or simple?

> Don't forget to give your melody a name, and copyright it using the correct symbol!

Improving your melodies

As with all new skills, learning to write good melodies can take time. Let's look at some things to consider when writing melodies.

◆ Have you written the music clearly? How do your noteheads and stems look?

◆ How fast should it go, and how loud or soft? Choose a tempo marking for your melody, and add some dynamic markings.

Rewrite your melody on the stave below, paying attention to these considerations. Try to space everything evenly and clearly.

Shape and motion in melodies

A melody that stays too much on the same note will quickly become boring. Melodies do use **repeated notes**, but generally they are in motion, either up or down. Sometimes they jump, with large shifts in pitch, but for the most part a melody will flow in a smooth ascending or descending motion. We call this the **contour** or shape of a melody.

Melodies more often move by step than by **leaps**. **Steps** are small movements, typically from one note to the next. Here is a good example, from the middle of 'All through the night':

The shape of that melody is clear:

Composers sometimes find it helpful to make a free drawing of the *shape* of music they want, before composing it in detail.

Small leaps are quite common, large ones less so, though they can add drama to a melody. 'Somewhere Over the Rainbow' starts with a large leap, an **octave**. We'll learn about octaves in the next section.

Repeated notes can appear in melodies too. Here are two well-known examples:

from 'Ode to Joy'

from 'Au clair de la lune'

Octaves and the Scale of C major

Use your piano keyboard. Find two Cs, using the diagram to guide you. (Clue: you need to look at the black notes to be sure of finding the right white notes!)

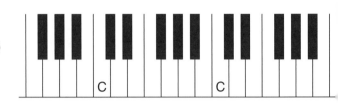

Place your right thumb on the lower C and your pinkie on the C above it. This may feel like a stretch at first, but this is how you play an octave leap.

Octaves are an **interval** or gap of 8 notes (counting both the top and bottom notes). Octaves are often used by composers to add excitement, played together or as a leap from one note to the other.

Here is the **scale of C major**, written over two octaves.

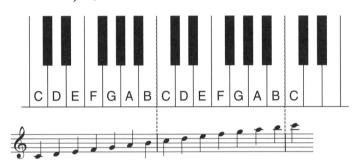

Composing task in C major

Name _____ Date _____

Your task is to create an 8-bar melody in 3/4 time.

Follow these steps to create your musical masterpiece. Tick them off as you complete them.

1 Explore some ideas for rhythm patterns, include at least one rest. ☐

2 Develop your rhythm ideas into a melody, writing an initial draft first. Add a treble clef to the stave, barlines and a double barline, and the 3/4 time signature. ☐

3 Make the first four bars one phrase and the second four bars an **answering phrase**. ☐

4 Use the notes of the C major scale. ☐

5 Your first and last notes should be C. ☐

6 Use a long note value for your final note. ☐

7 Add a tempo marking and dynamics. ☐

8 Choose a title for your melody and protect it using a copyright symbol. ☐

Initial rhythm ideas

$\frac{3}{4}$

Initial draft melody

Title _____

Appraise your composition by playing and listening back. Apply any changes you can make to improve how your melody sounds.

Final version

Title _____

Evaluate your learning in this chapter. List what stuck with you and new key words.

Form

Form in music refers to the structure or plan of a piece. Composers use the compositional skills we have been learning about when creating their works, but for large-scale pieces they usually follow a plan or format to give their work structure.

In Chapter 15, starting on page 65, we learned about form and 'music maps', diagrams to represent the structure or form of a piece of music. In relation to Kodály's 'The Viennese Musical Clock', we learned about **rondo form**. Look back at Chapter 15 to remind yourself about how several different pieces we listened to are structured.

Verse and chorus form

Most pop songs use **verse and chorus form**. Verses, with different words for each verse, alternate with choruses, which usually repeat the catchiest lines in the song, often including the title. Songs may include bridge sections or instrumental 'breaks' or solos. The repetition created by the verse/chorus format allows us to become familiar with the song.

Phrases

The 4-bar melodies we have been working on are also known as musical **phrases**. A phrase is like a sentence or statement; it expresses an idea.

When describing how a melody progresses we often use letters to represent where there is repetition or contrast in what we hear. When summarising the form of a piece of music in this way, we normally assign the letter **A** to indicate the first phrase. If the next phrase uses the same melody we add another **A** to show the **repetition**. However, if the melody is contrasting we will use B instead, to indicate the presence of a new melody.

Sing the following songs and discuss the phrase plan. Record the form using letters.

Song title	Form/Phrase plan
Twinkle twinkle little star	
All through the night	
My Bonnie lies over the ocean	
Continue with your own choice of songs	

Research definitions for these common forms

Binary Form	
Ternary Form	
Rondo Form	

Binary form has two contrasting phrases. **Ternary form** can also be described as **ABA form**. 'Twinkle twinkle little star' is an example of ternary form. Follow the melody on the staves below to identify the contrasting and repeated melodies used in this song.

Work with another student to create a melody with two 4-bar phrases. Decide what form or plan you will follow before you begin. Record your melody on the staves below.

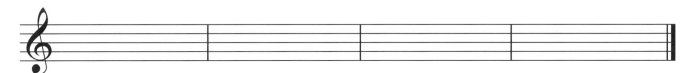

Collaborate to input your creation using technology software. Play back your melody and evaluate your composition. Is your form plan easily identified?

Accompaniment

When an **ensemble** or group of musicians perform a song, instruments which do not play the main melody or tune are instead **accompanying** it. Instruments which are suited to playing rhythmic patterns, harmonic patterns like **chords** or bass notes, are often used to provide accompaniment in performances.

Name four instruments that are regularly used to accompany performances

Chords

A chord is three or more notes played simultaneously to create harmony.

Composing with texture

Adding an accompaniment to a melody has the effect of adding another layer to enrich the **texture** of the music. Texture is an important feature of any piece of music, as we learned in Chapter 14. Texture describes what's going on in a piece of music, in terms of the layers in the music and what they do. A piece of music may have one melody, with or without accompaniment, many interwoven melodies or a supportive melody (or **countermelody**) designed to enhance the main melody. All these are different textures.

Can you recall the names of the three main types of texture in music and how we defined them? Look back at Chapter 14 to remind yourself about what we learned.

Monophonic	
Homophonic	
Polyphonic	

Most **homophonic** music consists of a melody with an added accompaniment. The accompaniment can be provided in many different ways but should not distract the listener from the one clear melodic line.

Guitars or keyboards are most often used to provide accompaniment to the singer's main melody. They may use chords or other patterns to enhance the vocal melody.

Questionnaire

Explain musical accompaniment.

_____

Identify instruments commonly used to accompany melodies.

_____

Propose the kind of music these instruments play.

_____

In your opinion, does accompaniment enhance a performance? _____

Comment on the **skills** required for musicians who play accompaniments.

_____

Ostinatos

'Mars' is one movement from a seven-movement work called *The Planets* by English composer Gustav Holst. Each movement has a subtitle, and this one is 'the bringer of war'. Listening to it, can you imagine why?

'Mars' from *The Planets* by Holst

Listen to the <u>opening section</u> of 'Mars'. Can you hear a **rhythmic motif** or idea that continues unchanging throughout this opening section? This type of repeated pattern is called an **ostinato**, from an Italian word meaning 'obstinate'.

An ostinato may be a rhythmic pattern or a short melody. Ostinatos are often used by composers as accompaniments. Look at the rhythmic ostinato used by Holst for 'Mars' below.

Listen again, and follow the ostinato pattern.

If you enjoyed the first section of 'Mars', and are interested to listen to the rest of the piece, you can find it on CD or online. You will easily hear that it is a good example of **ternary form**. In the middle section the character of the music changes; then it returns to the music of the opening.

Other examples of ostinatos to listen to:

Bolero by Ravel

'Viva La Vida' by Coldplay

'Money' by Pink Floyd

'Take Five' by Dave Brubeck

In 'Mars', the violin players use the wooden part of their bow – the 'stick' – to tap on the strings.

Name this performing technique

_____

_____

Composing a rhythmic ostinato

Experiment, using a percussion instrument to compose a short rhythmic pattern. Write it on the rhythm line below. Don't forget to write in the time signature, whichever one you have chosen.

Now compose a melody to go with your ostinato. Remember, your melody can be as long as you like, because the ostinato keeps repeating.

Using technology software available to you, input your work choosing suitable melody and rhythm instruments to play your parts. Listen back and evaluate your composition.

What stuck with you?

Evaluate your learning in this chapter. List what stuck with you and new key words.

Orchestral Scores

Great composers such as Mozart, Beethoven and Mahler often sketched their melodies quite roughly onto paper during the early stages of the creative process. Then, in order for other musicians to play their music accurately, they needed to organise their sketches into an accurate **musical score**, where all the details are set out. After that, performing parts can be made for each instrument to play from. The score includes *all* the parts, showing how they fit together, and is used by the **conductor**.

A page from Beethoven's notebooks

Examine the score shown opposite, which is the first page of the Trepak Russian dance from *The Nutcracker* by Tchaikovsky. Then listen to it on the CD.

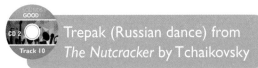

Trepak (Russian dance) from
The Nutcracker by Tchaikovsky

The score looks complicated, but the main tune is in the 1st violins. Try to follow it as you listen to the first few moments.

Points to notice:

◆ Although Tchaikovsky was Russian, everything in the score is written in Italian, including the names of the instruments.

◆ The sections of the orchestra are always written in this order

  ◆ Woodwinds at the top

  ◆ Brass ('corni' are horns)

  ◆ Percussion (with the tambourine written on a single-line stave, like the ones we used earlier)

  ◆ Strings

◆ The time signature is 2/4

What stuck with you?

Evaluate your learning in this chapter. List what stuck with you and new key words.

Graphic Scores

In recent times contemporary composers have developed new ways of notating their compositions for performers to play them. This is due to the use of new sounds like electronic sounds, found sounds and noises, and unconventional ways of playing instruments ('extended techniques').

One way of representing such sounds in a score is by making **graphic scores** which include shapes, drawings, symbols, text instructions, fragments of music notation and whatever else the composer wishes to add to the mix.

Graphic notation emerged in the 1950s, enabling the performance of music which cannot be notated using standard notation. Some graphic scores give a degree of freedom to the players, providing a starting point from which they have to use their own imagination and musical skill to perform. Such scores are one way for composers and performers to **collaborate** on the work or for performers to **improvise** within limits set by the composer.

Graphic scores are also employed to facilitate **chance** within the performance, so that no two performances will be the same.

Improvisation

When performers improvise, they are creating or performing music spontaneously or without prior preparation to produce or make something using chords, sequences, rhythms or other parameters indicated by the composer.

Creating graphic scores

There are no clear-cut rules to follow when creating a graphic score. Any of the following ideas might be used:

◆ The composer might complete a key, detailing what different elements in the score represent or how they should be played.

◆ They could represent sounds as shapes, dots, lines or Xs.

◆ They might use lines of different lengths to represent the duration of sounds.

◆ Line-thicknesses might represent changes in dynamics.

◆ Shapes or lines which move up or down might indicate changes in pitch.

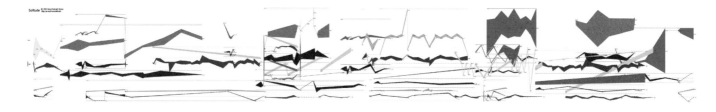

This graphic score was created by Hans-Christoph Steiner for his composition *Solitude*. It looks like a picture full of shapes and colours. The colours represent the different **sound samples** used by the composer. Time flows from left to right and pitch is represented vertically: high pitches towards the top of the frame and low pitches near the bottom.

Listen to the first three minutes of this five minute piece – and follow the score, if you can.

Solitude by Hans-Christoph Steiner

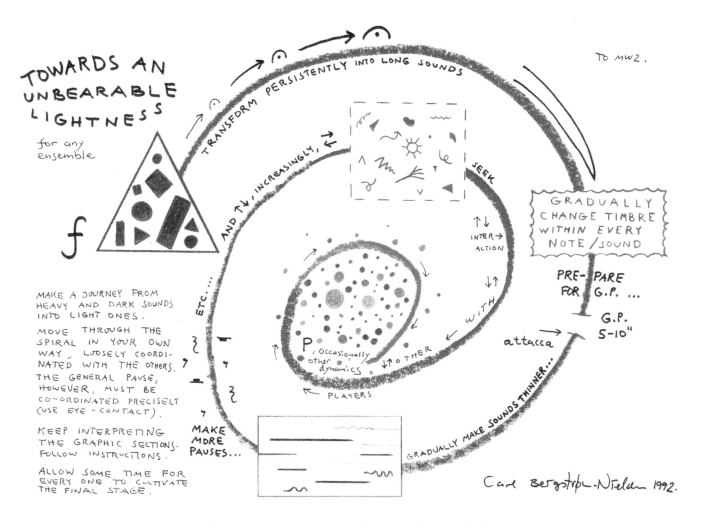

This spiral score was written by Carl Bergstrøm-Nielsen for his work *Towards An Unbearable Lightness*. The players start at the top left and work clockwise, following the instructions that appear on the left hand side. The composer writes:

> The score is a graphic representation of a journey from heavy dark sounds to light sounds. Players progress at their own rate through the spiral representing this change, loosely coordinating with the other players.

Cell notation

Another layout used to notate a graphic score is by breaking the composition into sections, presenting them in a series of cells or boxes. Each box holds information and the composition is performed one box at a time. For example:

Those are just examples of the sorts of symbols you could use. Think about the sounds you would make to match them.

Next, you will create your own graphic score, using this sort of method.

Create your own graphic score

A **sound source** is anything which generates vibrations to create a soundwave.

Working in groups, create and perform a graphic score of your own.

To get started we need some ideas. Do any of the images below provide inspiration? Choose one of them, or take an idea of your own.

Have you decided on your idea? Next, investigate different sound sources available to you: pencils, rulers, newspaper, other everyday objects. Or more unusual things – anything which generates vibrations to create a soundwave. You can use a musical instrument if you have access to one, but not necessarily played conventionally. Take time to explore what sounds are possible and how to control them.

Choose several sounds you feel will help you to illustrate the idea you have chosen. Decide what pattern or format your individual sounds could make; could they form a narrative, an overall shape?

Next, think about how your score should look. Identify the symbols or marks you will use to represent the sounds. Make a key like the one below, to explain to the performers what they should do.

Your choice of symbols	★★★★★★★ (stars)				
Instruction to players	Play lots of notes, gradually rising				

Rehearse the sounds each shape represents, and investigate what order works best when organising the layout of your composition. Try combining some of the sounds in different ways.

Compile and notate your group's composition in the chart below, inserting the symbols explained in your key. Make each cell last for 4 counts, so each of your sounds should be improvised to fit within those 4 beats.

Title _____ **Composer** _____

1 2 3 4	1 2 3 4		

© _____

Add a title and composer-credit at the top, and a copyright line at the bottom.

Performing your graphic score

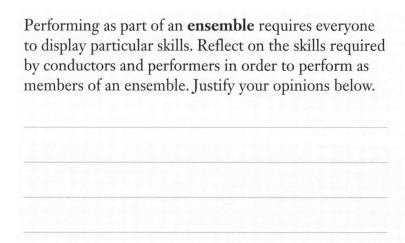

Once completed, choose one member of your group to be the **conductor**. Their role is to keep you performing together in time, using the conducting pattern for 4 beats per bar. Remember, each cell lasts for 4 beats. Rehearse together, and perform your piece to your classmates!

Performing as part of an **ensemble** requires everyone to display particular skills. Reflect on the skills required by conductors and performers in order to perform as members of an ensemble. Justify your opinions below.

_____

_____

_____

_____

Copyright

Copyright protects your intellectual property, preventing other people from reproducing it without your permission. Lyrics, poetry, images, music are all subject to copyright. When we compose a piece of music we can protect it by placing the © symbol at the end. Music recordings are protected by the ℗ symbol.

Is protecting your work important to you?

_____

Suggest two reasons why copyright is so important within the music industry.

(i) _____

(ii) _____

Found Sounds

Found sounds are the sounds made by found objects. Recording found sounds for use in music is something many experimental composers have done.

Did you use found sounds in your graphic score piece? If possible, record your **sound sources** to create a bank of found sounds. Then try manipulating your recorded sounds, for instance adding **reverberation**, and see what effects you can get.

Dogs barking, glasses clinking, hairdryer noise and bicycle bells have all been recorded for use in compositions. These are sounds which cannot easily be notated in standard notation and so are found in **graphic scores**.

John Cage

John Cage (1912–92) was a remarkable composer, and one of the early users of **graphic notation** and of **found sounds**. His most famous composition, written in 1952, was called *4'33"*. This piece required the pianist to sit at the piano for 4 minutes and 33 seconds but without playing a note. In the absence of sounds from the piano, the piece consists of the other sounds audible during the performance: environmental sounds of many sorts.

Another interesting composition by Cage is called *Cartridge Music*, composed in 1960. It is for 'amplified small sounds', made by small found objects, amplified by being inserted into the cartridge used to play a vinyl record.

Cage's *Roaratorio: Irish Circus on Finnegan's Wake* (1979) features sounds he recorded on his travels around Ireland, including folk musicians, blended into a collage with readings from James Joyce's book *Finnegan's Wake*, which had long fascinated Cage.

As an experimental composer, Cage was inspired by ideas such as facilitating **chance** and **improvisation** in performance, and he loved using found sounds, noise and alternative instruments in his art!

The *Sonatas and Interludes* (1946–48) are for **prepared piano** – a piano that has been altered, following Cage's instructions, by fixing objects on or between many of the strings: screws, nuts and bolts, pieces of rubber and plastic. These transform the **pitch** and **timbre** of the affected notes, turning the piano into a uniquely varied percussion instrument. Most of the higher and lower notes are left unaltered.

In these pieces, Cage experimented with pitch, rhythm and timbre, using rests to provide silences from which emerge a spectrum of delicate and unusual sounds both melodic and percussive.

Listen to 'Sonata No. 6' from *Sonatas and Interludes* by John Cage

 Write notes on the elements of music you can identify.

Pulse and rhythm	
Pitch and melody	
Timbre	
Texture	
Your reaction to this piece	

Other modern composers

 Explore the work of other modern or experimental composers. Here are some possible names, listed below – you will find examples of their music online. Or you might discover someone else whose experiments with music interest you.

Matthew Herbert	Steve Reich	Anna Meredith	Henry Cowell
Morton Feldman	Gerald Barry	Judith Weir	Kate Whitley

Choose a piece of contemporary music and make a programme note for it. Include:

◆ A brief introduction to the composer

◆ Something about the story told in the music, if there is one

◆ The circumstances surrounding the composition and why the composer chose to write this music

◆ The voices or instruments involved

◆ Interesting musical points to listen out for

◆ Your favourite section of the piece, and why

Compile a playlist of four contemporary pieces. List them below, giving the reasons why you have chosen these pieces.

Playlist title			
	Title	Composer	Reason for your choice
1			
2			
3			
4			

What stuck with you?

Evaluate your learning in this chapter. List what stuck with you and new key words.

In this units we have experienced and developed compositional skills. You now have a greater understanding of the creativity needed to compose music.

It isn't easy to make a living from composing, but there are possibilities. Our days are filled with music, all around us.

A job in the music industry you may not have considered is a jingle writer. Commercial jingle writers compose music for the adverts or commercials that we hear on radio or see on TV or online. **Jingles** are written explicitly to promote a product and to make the customer think of that product. Major brands use marketing agencies to design a new advert or campaign. Generally these will have music in them, and composers are employed to write this type of music.

The composer will be given a **brief** with details of what the **brand** is looking for. Can you think of some information that might be included in this brief?

_____

_____

You might be surprised how many jingles you know. Think of one and try to perform it. Notice how well you know the rhythm and melody and also the brand or product the jingle is connected to. Jingles can be fun, catchy – and sometimes annoying when they get stuck in our heads. (But anything that catchy must be good advertising!)

Name some successful adverts. _____

What impact can a jingle have on listeners? _____

Composing a jingle

In groups, let's compose our own jingle. Complete the following steps.

1 Choose a product or, better still, invent one.

_____

2 Create a brief. Include a logo, and briefly describe the message which will feature in your campaign for this product.

_____

_____

_____

3 Identify the mood you want your jingle to convey.

_____

_____

4 Compose the words for your jingle. It should be short and to the point.

_____

5 Compose a rhythm pattern that will carry the lyrics used in your jingle. Clapping back the rhythm pattern will help you to evaluate if it works well. Apply the lyrics under the rhythm notes.

6 When you are happy with your rhythm, try improvising some melodies. What sounds good when you sing it aloud?

7 Work together to identify the notes you are singing. Use any instruments available to help you do this. Write your melody on the stave below, and include the lyrics underneath.

8 Present your campaign to the class, describing your brief and how you feel you have met it.

 9 Perform your jingle for your classmates.

10 Reflect on the experience and how you feel your composing skills have helped you to complete this task.

_____

_____

_____

_____

What stuck with you?

Evaluate your learning in this chapter. List what stuck with you and new key words.

Reflection and Evaluation Sheet

Unit title:

Music I listened to:

Learning

Learning and exploring

I really enjoyed…

Something interesting I learned…

I excelled at…

My biggest challenge was…

I overcame this by…

I would like to learn more about…

New key words

Skills I developed in this unit…

This unit reminded me of learning about…

Goal setting…
-
-
-

Rate your learning

Music of the World

In this unit

In this unit you will explore the indigenous music of Ireland. Irish music is a source for understanding our history and will inform your understanding of Irish musicians and composers. An awareness of your own cultural music enables you to participate in your community in a meaningful way. Being culturally engaged, aware and connected to your indigenous music will help you to develop your own cultural identity. In this unit we will rehearse and perform together to demonstrate our knowledge and understanding of the musical elements, instruments and techniques associated with Irish music.

Intended learning

Design a rhythmic accompaniment for the spoons, adapt and improvise your rhythm over a recording of Irish dance tunes.

Compare different interpretations or arrangements of a Irish traditional song, paying attention to musical elements and other influences.

1.3,
1.13
2.3, 2.4,
2.9, 2.11
3.1, 3.3,
3.7, 3.10,
3.11

Distinguish between the sonorities, ranges and timbres of selections of traditional Irish instruments; identify how these sounds are produced and propose their strengths and limitations in performance.

Collaborate with fellow students and peers to produce a playlist and a set of traditional Irish recordings to accompany a local historical event or community celebration.

Compare compositions by two or more Irish songwriters; explain and describe differences and similarities in the compositions.

Discuss the principles of music property rights and explain how this can impact on the sharing and publishing of traditional Irish music.

Explore the time allocated to Irish artists and performers on a variety of local or national Irish media and present these findings to your class.

'World music' is a term sometimes used to refer to the traditional or **folk music** of particular cultures, peoples or countries. Music is a reflection of culture, and all music genres began in a particular part of the world. To understand world music we must understand the role it plays in the cultures to which it belongs.

Much of the music around the world belongs to the **oral tradition**. Discuss what this might mean?

Comment on the role music plays in Irish culture today?

_____

_____

_____

World music uses instruments and voices, rhythm and melody, and human expression. Some parts of the world favour one of these elements over the others – for instance African music is strongly associated with dance. Rhythm features strongly, and many interesting rhythmic instruments are used in different African traditions. Rhythm patterns and melodies are often repeated, varied or improvised.

Drummers of the Pan African Orchestra performing in Accra, Ghana

Variation and improvisation

Define what is involved in **variation** and **improvisation**?

In pairs, compose a rhythmic pattern in 4/4. Rehearse it until you can both keep playing it, repeating it steadily as a background rhythm. Then take turns to improvise over it, varying your patterns but keeping it together with the background rhythm.

Aboriginal music of Australia

Aboriginal music has been preserved and passed on from one generation to the next through **oral tradition**. It is an ancient culture, stretching back at least 50,000 years. The didgeridoo and clapsticks are its traditional instruments. The Aboriginal people speak of having sung their world into existence, singing out the name of everything they met on their travels.

Following the European colonisation of Australia in the eighteenth century, the indigenous people were driven off their ancestral lands. Many were killed, and those who survived still face discrimination into the twenty-first century. Their indigenous songs, known as **clansongs** or songlines, detail clan or family histories. A general word for songs which tell stories like this is **ballads**.

The didgeridoo, pictured on the right, is a long wooden tube, played by vibrating the lips within the mouthpiece. Rhythmic effects can be injected by controlling the vibrations, and variations in **timbre** come from adjusting the shape of the mouth and tongue.

Aboriginal didgeridoo player, with traditional body paint

Fusions

Like most forms of world music, Aboriginal music has, over time, fused with other styles. **Fusion** is created by combining one music style with another.

Can you think of any other examples of fusion in music?

_____

_____

Ceremonial band, India

Researching world music

 Investigate the characteristics of another type of world music. Every part of the world, every culture, has its own music, its own songs and its own instruments.

Choose a part of the world which is reflected in your school community. Maybe one of your classmates is from an interesting part of the world. Do a presentation to the class. Can you obtain recordings to play or incorporate a performance?

 Outline the key points you will make in your presentation below:

_____

_____

_____

_____

_____

_____

Street band, Cuba

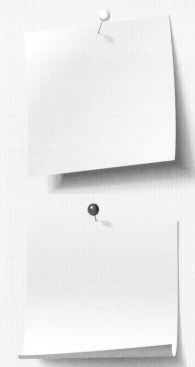

What stuck with you?

Evaluate your learning in this chapter. List what stuck with you and new key words.

Our Irish history is reflected in our traditional music. Like most forms of world music, Irish music began as an **oral tradition**. Ireland has long delighted in dance, music and song. Neighbours and families throughout Ireland gathered together by the fire in each other's homes to share their music. This sharing or passing on of our music from one generation to the next is understood as an **oral tradition**.

Young children learned and memorised their indigenous music by watching and listening to the older members in their family or community. For this reason, it is difficult to identify who composed many of our favourite traditional tunes, and there are many versions of traditional tunes in existence.

Can you name a piece of music from the Irish tradition that you learned at school?

Traditional songs

Ireland was also a land of poets and storytellers. Legends and folklore were part of every Irish childhood, also preserved through oral tradition. This craft of storytelling comes through in our ballads; our traditional songs are a treasure trove of Irish stories.

Can you name an Irish song which tells a story? _____

'Siúil a Rún'

This is a traditional song, known as a **lament**. The title translates as 'Go, my love' and tells the story of a woman lamenting the loss of her lover, who is going away to join the army.

Like many songs preserved through the oral tradition, we do not know who composed this song, and many versions exist. There are verses sung in both Irish and English. Songs using two languages like this are known as **macaronic**.

Listen to this song and describe its musical features in the grid below

Mood	
Tempo	
Dynamics	
Texture	
Rhythm	
Melody	
Other points of interest	

Acabella

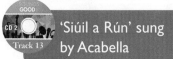

'Siúil a Rún' sung by Acabella

An American song called 'Johnny has Gone for a Soldier' which dates back to the American Revolution shares many of the same words and melody as 'Siúil a Rún'. Investigate possible reasons why Irish melodies and lyrics can often be found in American folk music.

'Siúil a Rún' is a lament. Research examples of these other types of songs in the Irish repertoire, completing the table below:

Type of song	Song title	Performer
Love song		
Lullaby		
Patriotic song		
Working songs		

'Ordinary Man'

'Ordinary Man' is a song by Peter Hames, made popular by the singer Christy Moore. Listen and interpret the story being told in this song. In pairs, explore the lyrics in this and other songs, and consider what they tell us about our culture and the kind of people we are.

'Ordinary Man'

Track 14

Christy Moore is a wonderful storyteller. He performed this song to the members of the Irish rugby team in preparation for the Grand Slam final against England in 2018. Ireland Coach Joe Schmidt quoted this song after Ireland's victory, saying his players were 'ordinary men, who are an extraordinary team'. Why do you think Christy Moore chose this song to perform for the players ahead of the game?

If you do a search online for 'Ordinary Man Christy Moore' you will find several different performances to listen to – the studio

Christy Moore

recording and some live performances. You can also find a recording of Peter Hames singing his own song, as well as other cover versions.

Listen to two different versions of 'Ordinary Man' and compare them. Do you have a preference, and why?

_____

_____

_____

Features of Irish music

Irish traditional music has many recognisable features. Learning about these helps us to appreciate it as a unique art form.

◆ Traditional Irish music is a *solo* art form. It was originally performed without accompaniment. Group performances provided music for dancing, but, for the most part, songs were performed solo, unique to the performer.

◆ Individual performers often use **ornamentation**, such as **grace notes** added between the main notes of the melody, to add interest and individuality to each performance.

◆ The tempo is controlled by the performer, guided by the expressive nature of the melody, slowing down or speeding up as the performer feels is needed. There is sometimes no clear or definite pulse or beat; we call this **free rhythm**.

◆ The melodic **range** tends to be wide. The pitch of Irish melodies often stretches high and low, depending on the needs or wishes of the individual performer. Certain notes of the scale can be left out. These are called **gapped scales**.

◆ The tonality of Irish music is mostly **modal**. Modal scales are a little different from major scales.

◆ Tunes and songs are composed using simple forms and structures. Performers often use a **repeated final note** as a way to indicate the end of a piece.

Irish music places much importance on storytelling. Performances use ornamentation, free rhythm and a wide melodic range to express the story, in preference to dynamics or formal complexity. Similarly, the use of classical devices such as **harmony** or **polyphony** are rare. Features such as dynamics, harmony and accompaniment are sometimes used in performances of Irish music but are then considered to be **non-traditional** features of the performance.

Mary Black

Complete the diagram below by inserting key words used to describe the traditional features of Irish music.

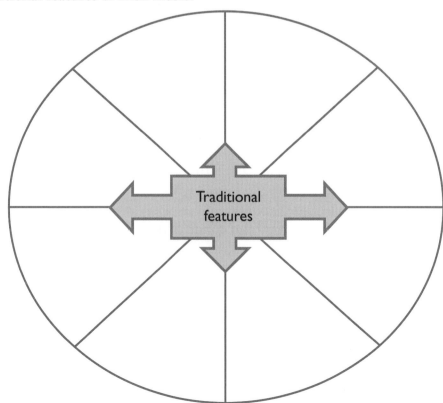

Comparing different performances of a song

'The Parting Glass'

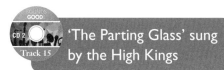

'The Parting Glass' sung by the High Kings

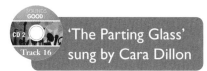

'The Parting Glass' sung by Cara Dillon

Listen to two versions of 'The Parting Glass', a well-known Irish **lament**.

Work in pairs to compare these two interpretations of this song, and consider how the elements of music have been varied. Evaluate the two performances and identify the skills and techniques used.

The High Kings performing during a concert in Berlin

Compare and contrast One song – two interpretations		
Song title		**Style**
Version 1 performers		**Version 2 performers**
Special to version 1	**Common elements**	**Special to version 2**

Performing 'The Parting Glass'

Here are the lyrics of verse 1 of this beautiful song.

Consider the features of traditional performance – ornamentation, free rhythm, solo performance – and apply them as you see fit. Rehearse and perform a verse of this song for your classmates.

List **traditional features** of your performance below:

_____

_____

_____

Of all the money that e'er I had
I spent it in good company
And all the harm that e'er I've done
Alas, it was to none but me
And all I've done for want of wit
To memory now I can't recall
So fill to me the parting glass
Good night and joy be with you all

Sean-nós

Sean-nós means 'old style'. This pure style of traditional singing probably dates back hundreds of years, surviving through oral tradition. It is often highly ornamented. The style of sean-nós performance varies from one part of the country to another.

Listen to an example of sean-nós singing.

 'Na Páipéir á Saighneáil' sung by Eimear Arkins

This is an old song from the west of Ireland. Its theme is like that of 'Siúil a Rún', a lament for a lover departing for war.

Sean-nós singing demands skill and an ability to **improvise**. It exemplifies the traditional features we have noted before:

◆ Storytelling: words are given prominence over melody and rhythm.

◆ Sean-nós singers perform **unaccompanied**.

◆ **Free rhythm** allows the natural flow of the words.

◆ Sean-nós singers do not use dynamics to add emotion to their performances, preferring to maintain an even tone throughout. Using dynamics is thought to distract from the music: moments of intensity are instead represented either by the addition of ornamentation or by stripping the lyrics back to the utmost simplicity.

◆ Sean-nós singers rarely sing anything the same way twice. **Ornamentation** is chosen by the performer and puts a unique stamp on their style of performing. Variations of rhythm and melody may also occur.

◆ **Melisma** is used to add embellishment. Adding many notes per **syllable** ornaments the song for the performer.

◆ Singers sometimes use a nasal tone or lengthen or emphasise particular sounds.

◆ Occasionally nonsense syllables are added to the lyrics.

Listen again to the singing of Eimear Arkins. Which of the traditional features mentioned above are represented in her performance?

_____

_____

_____

_____

_____

_____

'Casadh an tSúgáin' (A Twist of the Rope)

An example of sean-nós singing features in the 2015 film *Brooklyn*, based on a novel by Colm Tóibín. Set in 1951, a fragment of this haunting song is heard – sung by Iarla Ó Lionáird as the character Frankie – in a scene depicting Irish immigrants enjoying Christmas dinner at a soup kitchen in Brooklyn. The song adds a deeply nostalgic quality to the scene.

To see this scene from the film, search online for 'Casadh an tSúgáin Iarla Ó Lionáird Brooklyn'. As with the performance by Eimear Arkins, identify the traditional features in Ó Lionáird's performance.

_____   _____

_____   _____

_____   _____

Aislingí

An **aisling** (pl. aislingí) is a patriotic song or poem which identifies Ireland as a woman, lamenting the current political state of Ireland, and predicts a revival of Ireland's fortunes.

'Táimse im' Chodhladh'

Listen to two performances of this well-known aisling.

CD 2 Track 18 · 'Táimse im' Chodhladh' sung by Dolores Keane

CD 2 Track 19 · 'Táimse im' Chodhladh' sung by Zoë Conway

Compare and contrast the two performances, using the Venn diagram in the teacher's book to write up your results.

Dolores Keane

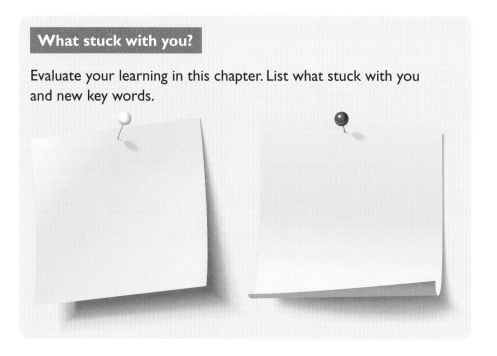

What stuck with you?

Evaluate your learning in this chapter. List what stuck with you and new key words.

Zoë Conway

Traditional Irish instrumental music has many of the same features as the vocal music, such as ornamentation. The oldest style of instrumental performance is called a **slow air**. The melody was often taken from a sean-nós song, performed on traditional instruments such as whistle, flute or fiddle, using the same techniques and features as a sean-nós singer.

Tin whistle

The tin whistle is also known as a **feadóg stáin** or a **penny whistle**. Of all the instruments used in traditional Irish music, the whistle is possibly the most played. This inexpensive instrument has six holes, a plastic mouthpiece, and a range of two **octaves**. Many traditional musicians began by learning to play the tin whistle before moving on to other more complex instruments. Most tin whistles are pitched in the key of D, and much traditional music is written in this key signature.

Popular tin whistle players include Mary Bergin and Paddy Maloney. Listen to Mary Bergin performing a slow air called 'Aisling Gheal'.

'Aisling Gheal' played by Mary Bergin

Do you think this performance on tin whistle shares similar features with the sean-nós vocal performances we have listened to? What similarities and what differences did you hear?

_____

_____

_____

Compare the upper photograph showing the playing position with the photograph of Mary Bergin. Do you notice something unusual?

Yes, Mary Bergin plays 'left-handed' – that is, with her right hand at the top, contrary to the usual way of playing instruments in the flute and recorder families.

Mary Bergin

The collecting of 'Aisling Gheal'

The tune 'Aisling Gheal' was collected by Alexander Martin Freeman in Cork in 1914. He notated the melody, thereby ensuring its preservation. We will learn more about the influence and importance of collecting music in this way later in this chapter.

Researching Irish instruments

 Investigate and make notes on the following traditional instruments. Include information on pitch, range and timbre and the instrument's strengths and limitations. Refer to a well-known performer in each case.

Instrument	Description	Well-known player
Tin whistle		
Low whistle		
Irish flute		
Fiddle		
Accordion		
Concertina		
Uilleann pipes		
Harp		
Bodhran		
Bones		
Spoons		

Choose a well-known performer you have listened to while compiling your research. Detail the traditional features you have identified during their performances.

Performer	Instrument
Style	
Traditional features used	**Non-traditional features**
Outline what you like about this performer's way of playing.	
Describe how the music made you feel.	

Playing the Spoons

Historically, this fun-to-play folk instrument was mastered by almost all traditional musicians. Playing spoons as an instrument originated long ago, but it requires us to develop new skills and **improvise** rhythmically over the tunes played by the melody instruments.

◆ Take two spoons of similar shape and size: soup spoons are a good option. To start with, place one in each hand, and practise striking the table to create interesting rhythm patterns. Stick to a pulse of 4 to keep things steady, but use your creative skills to build or improvise your rhythms. Play along with some recordings of traditional Irish music and see what kind of rhythms and sounds you can produce.

◆ Now hold both spoons in one hand with the convex surfaces meeting. Grip them firmly, with the first finger keeping the handles apart.

◆ Keeping your spoons parallel, try striking your knee, and you will begin to hear the rhythmic sounds take shape. This takes practice, but, once you have mastered it, you will be able to strike the spoons off your palm, fingers, knee or other objects to create your clacking rhythmic sounds.

◆ Sitting, hold your spoons above one knee and your other hand above the spoons, palm facing down. Practise striking down to your knee and back up to bounce off your palm.

Spoons are classed as **idiophones** – instruments which produce sound directly, usually through being struck or scraped. Not all sets of spoons sound the same. The composition, size and shape determine the sonority and pitch.

Advanced players perfect a form of **ornamentation** called a **roll**. To do this, stretch the fingers of your opposite hand with the thumb facing upwards. Keeping your fingers outstretched and stiff, pass the spoons along your fingers from top to bottom, ending by striking your knee. This creates the sound of a drum roll. Try it!

Playing the spoons is difficult at first. It takes time to develop your grip, and the spoons wobble around as you try to strike them. But with practice you can perfect this skill.

To develop your new skills, try to accompany some of the traditional music we have listened to during this chapter. Improvise to create a rhythmic pattern which works with the piece of music you have chosen.

Rehearse and present a short rhythmic accompaniment for a piece of traditional music using the spoons.

Playing the spoons at St Patrick's Day Parade, London

Group Playing – Céilí Bands

Irish music, as we have seen, was originally a solo activity. **Sean-nós** and **slow air** traditions gave singers and players freedom to perform each piece as they wished. This allowed the creative personality of the individual performer to shine through. In more recent times, traditional musicians have increasingly wished to come together to play music. Nowadays it is very common to hear two or three traditional instruments playing together.

Seamus Clandillon was a civil servant, teacher and singer. In 1926 he was appointed director of broadcasting on the first Irish radio station, called 2RN but later named Radio Eireann. He encouraged groups of musicians to play together for dancing, and these groups of musicians became known as **céilí bands**.

Four Courts Céilí Band, 1962

Dances were traditionally held at the crossroads of rural villages. The Dance Hall Act of 1935 resulted in these gatherings occurring in parochial halls throughout the country. Céilí musicians provided the music. Maintaining a strict rhythm, projecting the music so it could be heard in a large hall and performing the melody in unison were the important features of their performances.

 Well-known céilí bands include the Tulla Céilí Band or the Kilfenora Céilí Band. Write a note about one of these or about a céilí band of your own choice.

_____

_____

_____

_____

Knockmore Céilí Band at the Fleadh Cheoil 2014, Sligo

Dance Music of Ireland

Ireland is recognised around the world for its traditional dancing. No culture exists without dance, and in Ireland it is central to our heritage, like our language and our national sports. We have been very successful in preserving it for future generations.

Irish dancing began with the Celts, and many rituals and celebrations centred around dancing. Events known as **feiseanna** (plural – singular **feis**) celebrated art, music, storytelling and other traditions. Feiseanna are still important events for traditional dancers today.

By the eighteenth century, Irish dancing as we know it had begun to take shape, with specific structures and forms. Dance masters travelled round rural villages, and solo dancers displayed their skill. Dancing was accompanied by harp, pipes or singing. Nowadays many more instruments are included in ceili bands. Ornate costumes are often worn.

The Irish Dancing Commission was set up in 1930 and has managed all areas of this tradition since then. It began hosting the World Championships in 1970, and today this competition sees over 7,000 dancers enter from all corners of the world. A seven-minute interval act performed for the Eurovision Song Contest in 1994 led to the theatrical phenomenon known as *Riverdance*, bringing unprecedented levels of popularity to Irish dance.

Form in Irish dances

Irish dances have a common **form** or structure that allows dancers to match their steps to the music. The main dances in the Irish repertoire are **reels**, **hornpipes** and **jigs**.

Irish dances are typically 32 bars long and follow a form referred to as a **round** – though this should not be confused with the polyphonic type of round in which one voice follows another (see page 62).

There are two parts within the 32 bar dance, and each part is 16 bars long. Each part has an 8 bar **phrase** which is repeated. The first part is known as the **tune** (A) and the second part as the **turn** (B).

Structure of Irish dance tunes

Tune		Turn	
A	A	B	B
8 bars	8 bars	8 bars	8 bars

'Cooley's Reel'

Listen carefully to identify the form of this dance as AABB. Can you hear the tune (A) and the turn (B)? What do you notice about the pitch of the melody in the turn?

Listen again, following the score. There are three performances: plain, then ornamented, then using **low whistle**. Mark places where you can hear that the performer has added ornamentation. Use different coloured pens for each performance.

> 'Cooley's Reel' played in three different ways by Neil Moloney on low whistle and Evan O'Sullivan on tin whistle

Recognising Irish dance tunes

Today most Irish dance tunes are performed in a concert setting or at festivals such as the Fleadh Cheoil. Dance tunes are performed for listening to more than for dancing; for this reason, the tempo and rhythmic features which typically help us to identify our traditional dances can be less obvious.

Of the three most popular dances within our tradition, **jigs** are the oldest, with double jigs the most common. **Reels** are fast, and popular with musicians. **Hornpipes** are slower, making them a popular choice with dancers hoping to showcase their most complicated steps.

> Research the Fleadh Cheoil and identify the location of the festival this year.
>
> _____
>
> _____

Dance types

In pairs or groups, research the three types of dance listed. Collate your findings and complete the table below. You will need to identify the time signature for each type of dance, a typical bar of rhythm, and an example to listen to.

Type of dance	Origin	Time signature	Typical bar of rhythm	Example
Reel				
Hornpipe				
Jig				

'Off to California' CD 2 Track 22

'The Banshee' CD 2 Track 23

'Out on the Ocean' CD 2 Track 24

Listen to these three dances. Identify the type of dance (reel, hornpipe or jig) and the instruments used.

	Type of dance	Instruments used
1		
2		
3		

Harp Music

While Irish music and dance were historically passed from one generation to the next through **oral tradition**, we have developed ways of preserving and protecting our music heritage.

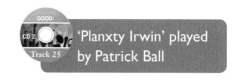

'Planxty Irwin' played by Patrick Ball

This began with harp music. The harp holds a special importance within Irish culture. Harpers were respected and prestigious musicians, employed under **patronage** by the Irish aristocracy. Harpers composed and performed music for their **patrons**, for special events such as birthdays or weddings. They called these pieces **planxties** – typically lively tunes composed and dedicated to the harper's patron using their family name. Listen to this example, 'Planxty Irwin', written by Turlough O'Carolan.

Following English rule, patrons no longer lived in the great houses and castles. Harpers lost their jobs, and those that remained travelled round Ireland seeking work where they could.

Research the life and music of Turlough O'Carolan, one of the last travelling harpers. Indicate your findings below:

Moya Brennan of Clannad, performing at Lorient (Brittany), 2013

_____

_____

_____

_____

What stuck with you?

Evaluate your learning in this chapter. List what stuck with you and new key words.

By the 1700s harp music was in real decline, and Ireland was in danger of losing the harping heritage. The process of notating harp music, and thus preserving the tunes, began at the Belfast Harp Festival in 1792. A young man named Edward Bunting, an experienced organist, was employed to take notes at the festival, and he wrote down the melodies, also making notes on the way the harpers played.

This began the important process of notating and preserving Irish melodies. Bunting spent the rest of his life travelling round Ireland, listening to musicians in rural communities and notating their music, making collections of tunes which he later published in books. Today, if we want to learn how to play 'Planxty Irwin' or 'Aisling Gheal', we can easily access sheet music in shops or online due to the work of Edward Bunting and other collectors.

Another collector was Francis O'Neill, a Cork man who emigrated to America in the mid 1800s and collected tunes from the Irish diaspora he met in Chicago.

We have mentioned the collecting of 'Aisling Gheal' by Alexander Martin Freeman in 1914. Later, another influential figure was the composer, arranger and teacher Seán ÓRiada, who did much to promote the revival of Irish traditional music in the 1960s, especially in ensemble formats.

Investigate the role of the collectors, and complete the questions below.

1 Consider why the work of collectors was so important.

_____

_____

2 Propose why there was new music for O'Neill to collect in Chicago.

_____

_____

3 Consider the songs he collected, suggest what the lyrics might have been about.

_____

_____

4 If you were to begin collecting Irish music today, what parts of the world would be worth researching and why?

_____

_____

5 Identify the formats you would use to collect information.

_____

_____

6 Evaluate how collecting music has changed since the time of Bunting and O'Neill.

_____

_____

7 Detail what is involved in preserving Irish music today.

_____

_____

8 Describe some of the developments which have been made in recording new music.

_____

_____

9 Discuss the impact this has on individual performers and the Irish music repertoire.

_____

_____

Copyright and traditional music

Copyright law protects artistic creators. By its traditional nature, it might seem that Irish music might not be protected by copyright laws: we can't trace the original composers in many cases.

Other difficulties arise around **ornamentation**; variation and embellishment are an integral part of Irish performance. However, if a musician makes a recording, with the addition of ornamentation, copyright law can protect both the original composition, if a composer has been established, and the new recording.

Most copyright protection lasts for the lifetime of the composer plus 70 years after they have died. After that, the music is available for use in the 'public domain', and performers can use and alter the music as they wish.

Many composers have respectfully taken compositions no longer protected by copyright and used them as the inspiration or basis of their own compositions. For example, contemporary composer Gerald Barry uses Turlough O'Carolan's tune 'Sí bheag, sí mhór' as part of his Piano Quartet No.1, first performed in London in 1992.

What stuck with you?

Evaluate your learning in this chapter. List what stuck with you and new key words.

Irish music has developed in many ways over the past hundred years:

◆ The development of group playing in the ceili tradition

◆ The introduction of other folk instruments into the tradition, such as banjo and guitar

◆ Performers using non-traditional features such as accompaniment or harmony

◆ Emigration and immigration which has introduced performers to new experiences and a blending of ideas and traditions, sometimes known as **fusion**

◆ The development of recording technology

◆ Increased availability, beginning with radio and television, and more recently including music streaming and on-demand sourcing of recordings

The last point on that list has led to a huge increase in fusions of different musical traditions. Irish music has successfully fused with styles such as rock, jazz, classical and popular music. Some people believe fusion has helped the revival in Irish music during the last 50 years; others feel it has diluted our tradition, making it less pure.

'Buaile Mo Chroi'

Listen to this example of traditional Irish music mixed with jazz influences.
The song was written by John Spillane, and is another example of a **macaronic song**.

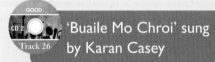

'Buaile Mo Chroi' sung by Karan Casey

With the help of your teacher, identify other examples of fusion and complete the information box below.

Type of fusion	Song title and performer	Traditional features	Non-traditional features

Irish music now reaches global audiences. By combining with other genres and cultures, we are making our music more accessible. Composers such as Seán Ó Riada, Bill Whelan and Sean Davy, and performers such as the Chieftains, Afro-Celt Soundsystem and, more recently Moxi, have had successful careers fusing Irish music with other styles.

Advances in technology, recording and even transport have also had a role to play. The globalisation of music and its instant accessiblity have placed Ireland in a wider context.

Compare and contrast **two** Irish composers whose compositions have been influenced by fusion. Research background information on the composers you choose, listen to one of their works and identify the differences and similarities between them. Summarise your findings below or in a venn diagram.

Rian ceoil

Rian ceoil is the Irish term for playlist. In groups, discuss any commemorative events or community celebrations which could require a playlist of Irish traditional music. List any events or celebrations you have identified here:

_____   _____

_____   _____

Together, decide on **one** of these and work together to produce a playlist of five songs to accompany the event.

Event or celebration: _____

Location: _____

Song Title	Performer	Style

What stuck with you?

Evaluate your learning in this chapter. List what stuck with you and new key words.

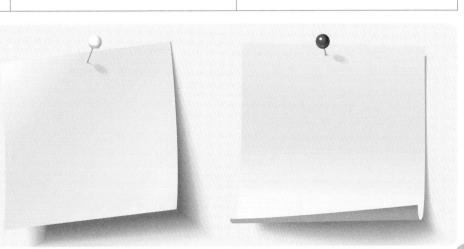

Reflection and Evaluation Sheet

Unit title:

Music I listened to:

Learning

Learning and exploring

I really enjoyed…

Something interesting I learned…

I excelled at…

My biggest challenge was…

I overcame this by…

I would like to learn more about…

New key words

Skills I developed in this unit…

This unit reminded me of learning about…

Goal setting…

-
-
-

Rate your learning

Performing

In this unit

Music performance is an enjoyable and collaborative activity. In this unit you will begin to develop the skills required for performance by engaging in activities such as body percussion, singing and sight reading. You will have an opportunity to bring your own creative ideas to life for performance. Rehearsing and performing together is a rewarding part of music making. You will gain experience in forms of sight-reading and aural memory singing. By exploring and participating in the activities in this unit you might notice your musical self has begun to shine.

Intended learning

Compose and perform or play back short musical phrases and support these phrases by creating rhythmic ostinati to accompany them.

Read, interpret and play from symbolic representations of sounds.

Perform music at sight through singing or clapping melodic and rhythmic phrases.

Rehearse and perform pieces of music that use common textures.

1.1,
1.5, 1.7,
1.8, 1.9
2.1, 2.5,
2.10

Demonstrate an understanding of a range of metres and pulses through the use of body percussion or other means of movement.

Experiment and improvise with making different types of sounds on a sound source and notate a brief piece that incorporates the sounds by devising symbolic representations for these sounds.

Prepare and rehearse a musical work for an ensemble focusing on cooperation and listening for balance and intonation.

Develop a set of criteria for evaluating a live or recorded performance; use these criteria to complete an in-depth review of a performance.

Do you ever feel chills down your spine while listening to music? Music is powerful stuff! Every performance has a little magic to share with you, whether you are listening to the music or actually making it – playing or singing.

Performing takes you straight to the centre of the magic. Everyone is a performer in the making, and in this unit we will explore performing and develop our performance skills.

Creating music engages many parts of the brain! It increases memory, coordination and physical agility. It develops our organisational skills but, most importantly, provides us with a chance to work together.

The earliest visual images of musical performance are inscribed on rock paintings and excavated objects. Music was part of ritual in early cultures; music was performed for dancing, working and many day-to-day activities. Early instruments were mainly percussive or flute-like instruments, made from bones or wood. Singing is the oldest musical activity of all, an important form of expression. No culture has existed without music performance.

The world's oldest instrument was found during an excavation of an early Bronze Age mound in Wicklow, in 2003. The find consisted of six carefully crafted wooden pipes.

Made from yew wood, they were discovered lying side by side, in descending order: longest to shortest. Can you guess why they were different lengths?

They are known as the Wicklow Pipes and are believed to date from 2200–2000BC.

 Research! Can you find out information on other ancient Irish instruments?

STOMP is a rhythmic phenomenon which combines body percussion, dance and comedy to create an energetic show making something really extraordinary from ordinary things! It has been a global sensation, on stage for over 25 years. Masterminds Luke Cresswell and Steve Mc Nicholas

created theatrical magic using objects like newspapers and sweeping brushes.

Search for STOMP online, and watch these performances:

◆ 'Just clap your hands'   ◆ 'Newspapers'

Performing is more enjoyable with company. Creating music with your classmates means we must work together as a team; listening to each other will be very important. Performing together will improve teamwork skills and discipline. In order for an **orchestra** to sound good, all the players must work together towards a single goal. To do this, they must commit to learning the music, attending rehearsals, and practising between rehearsals.

Singing

A wise teacher once said 'If you can talk, you can sing'. What do you think?

There are many positive side-effects to singing with friends. Can you name five benefits of singing? Why does it make people feel great?

This is what Fred said:

1	
2	
3	
4	
5	

Hi, my name is Fred. I started singing with my school friends in school last year. I never miss a rehearsal, even though in the beginning I wasn't sure I would enjoy it. I went along on the first day with my friend Tom and it was good fun.

I enjoy singing as it gives me a chance to express myself and always lifts my mood. Sometimes I like to write my own songs. Writing lyrics down on the page is a great way to write about my day, my feelings or life in general.

The feel-good effect

◆ When you sing, your body releases endorphins – hormones that energise you and make you feel good.

◆ Singing is good aerobic exercise. As you breathe in and out to sing, you calm your body and relieve any tension or stress. The deep breaths necessary for singing improve our lung function, increasing the oxygen in our bloodstream and boosting our immune system (see below).

◆ Your ears also get a workout! Singing with others involves listening to the different voices and training your musical ear.

◆ Singing is sharing. Coming together to perform as a choir is rewarding and fun. It gives us a sense of community, encouraging friendship and teamwork.

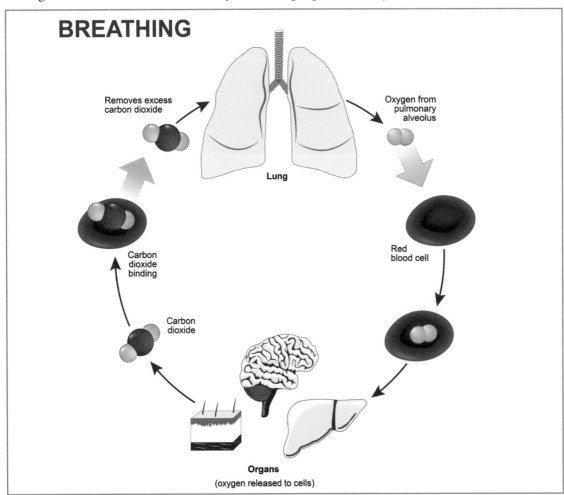

BREATHING

Removes excess carbon dioxide

Oxygen from pulmonary alveolus

Lung

Red blood cell

Carbon dioxide binding

Carbon dioxide

Organs
(oxygen released to cells)

What stuck with you?

Evaluate your learning in this chapter. List what stuck with you and new key words.

Warming up the Voice

Relax and loosen

First – just like anyone who takes part in sport – we should warm up. Stand up and shake off the day.

◆ Relax. Shake it out: hands, feet, arms, then legs.

◆ Roll your shoulders backwards, then forwards.

◆ Roll your head from side to side.

◆ Shake fingers, hands and wrists to loosen out.

Posture is important when we are singing. Stand up straight, shoulders down and relaxed.

Breathing and singing go hand in hand. Breathe from your diaphragm. Place your hand on your tummy: if you are breathing from your diaphragm you should feel your tummy rise and fall. Breathe in, then blow out, slowly and steadily.

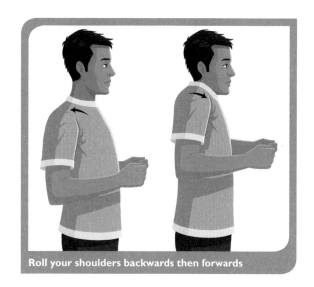

Roll your shoulders backwards then forwards

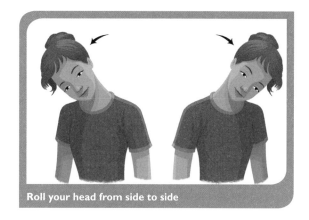

Roll your head from side to side

Humming

Humming is a great way to warm up. Let's hum the following lines from well-known melodies. Your teacher will play the first note for you. Listen to each other, and keep in time.

Mm mm mm mm mm mm, mm mm mm mm mm mm

Repeat several times, beginning a note higher each time.

Here's another one:

Mm mm mm mm mm mm mm mm mm mm mm mm

Vowel singing and other useful warm-up exercises

Singing vowel-sounds is another great way to get your voice ready to sing. We know the vowels for the English language are a, e, i, o, u, but how do they sound when we sing them?

Vowel	Sound when sung
a	ah (as in 'car')
e	e (as in 'get')
i	ee (as in 'week')
o	o (as in 'got')
u	oo (as in 'food')

The **e** sound is quite difficult to sing as a long sound because it's normally a short vowel-sound when spoken.

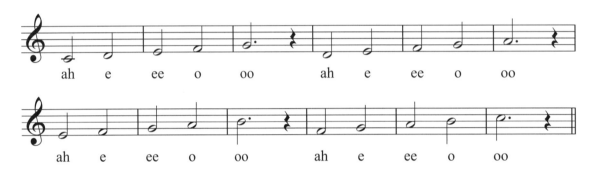

Other sounds are useful too. Try this one. Begin a note higher each time and hear how far your range can go.

My favourite one is this:

Or try it with these words:

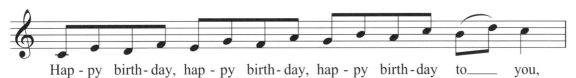

Hap - py birth - day, hap - py birth - day, hap - py birth - day to___ you,

Hap - py birth - day, hap - py birth - day, hap - py birth - day to___ you,

Compose your own warm-up lyrics to match this melody? Copy the melody onto the blank staves below and add your lyrics under the notes, taking care to align each syllable vertically under its note.

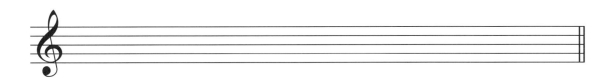

What stuck with you?

Evaluate your learning in this chapter. List what stuck with you and new key words.

Unison singing

Most of the singing we do in primary school is unison singing. The word unison comes from the Latin word *uni*, meaning one. It essentially means one melody. When thousands of people stand in the Aviva Stadium to sing our national anthem before an event, they are singing 'in unison'. Everyone sings the melody in the exact same way.

Let's try it. Here are the words:　**Sinne Fianna Fáil, atá faoi gheall ag Éirinn**

How did it sound? Were we all singing together? Unison singing is a great way to sing together!

Singing in harmony

Harmony is when two or more notes or pitches are sung together simultaneously.

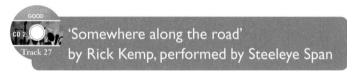

'Somewhere along the road'
by Rick Kemp, performed by Steeleye Span

Discuss how you felt about the song and the performance, and fill in the chart below to describe your opinions.

Title	Composer	Style
Somewhere along the road		
Texture	Dynamics	Tempo

What did you like about this performance? (Discuss the vocals and the accompaniment.)

How did the music make you feel?

'Somewhere along the road'

Listen again to the recording of 'Somewhere along the road', and follow the music notation below.

Rick Kemp

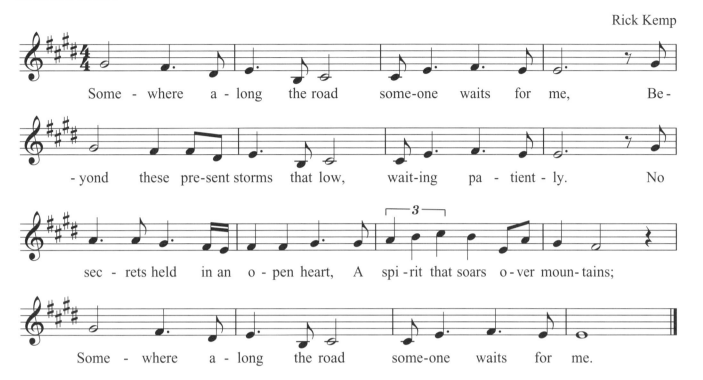

Some - where a - long the road some-one waits for me, Be -

- yond these pre-sent storms that low, wait-ing pa - tient - ly. No

sec - rets held in an o - pen heart, A spi-rit that soars o-ver moun-tains;

Some - where a - long the road some-one waits for me.

2 Somehow a guiding light always shows the way,
   To those who lose their way by night, searching for the day.
      A day away from happiness,
      Tomorrow will bring a new sunrise;
   Somewhere along the road someone
   waits for me.

3 Sometime when winds are still unexpectedly,
   Perhaps beyond this silent hill, a voice will
   call to me.
      Raise your eyes to see my world,
      Raise your voice and sing out;
   Somewhere along the road someone waits
   for me.

Steeleye Span

Rounds

Singing in harmony can be difficult to do at first, so a good place to begin is to sing a round.

A round is when we sing the same melody or song but begin at different times. Once we become confident with the melody and remember to work together as a team, we can sing in perfect harmony.

? Test yourself

What is the texture of a round?

_____

Discuss the reason for your answer.

'Row, row, row your boat'

Row, row, row your boat gent - ly down the stream.

Mer-ri - ly, mer-ri - ly, mer-ri - ly, mer-ri - ly, Life is but a dream.

Sing it in unison first. Then in two parts, with the second group starting when the first group reaches bar 5. Then try in three parts, then four, with the different groups **two bars apart**.

'Hava Nashira'

'Hava Nashira' is a beautiful song with a haunting melody. Singing this tune as a three-part round reveals beautiful harmonies. Its Hebrew lyrics translate to mean 'Let us sing together, sing alleluia'.

Ha - va na - shi - ra, shir hal - le - lu - ia!

Ha - va na - shi - ra, shir hal - le - lu - ia!

Ha - va na - shi - ra, shir hal - le - lu - ia!

Sight-reading, sight-singing

If you play an instrument and you perform a piece by reading the sheet music without having seen it before, we call that **sight-reading**. Sight-reading is an important skill for any performer. Musicians performing with an orchestra must have excellent sight-reading skills to help them play complex pieces of music, often with little time to prepare.

Sight-singing is a form of sight-reading – singing by reading the printed music. Think of your favourite songs. You know them really well, so you can sing them easily. But imagine that you had never heard a song and you were asked to perform it just by looking at the music. Tricky, right? One way that makes it easier is **tonic solfa**.

Tonic Solfa

Tonic solfa, also known as 'solfeggio singing', is a method of naming note pitches, and is widely used as a method of sight-singing. Most people know it from the song 'Do-Re-Mi', from the 1959 film *The Sound of Music* by Richard Rodgers and Oscar Hammerstein. However, the origins of tonic solfa go back much further, as far as the eleventh century!

Let's sight-sing the scale of C major, using the tonic solfa names.

Now sing it again, just from the solfa names, without the written notes:

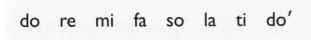

The dash after the last 'do' shows that it's high 'do', an octave higher than the starting note.

The scale we sang is **ascending**. But can you sing it **descending**? Let's try it.

do′ ti la so fa me re do

We can even shorten the solfa names to their initial letters. Sing the scale again, ascending and then descending.

d r m f s l t d′   d′ t l s f m r d

Now try these short exercises:

d m s m d
d m d m s m d
d′ t l s l t d′

Compose two more of your own, writing the solfa letters below.

1
2

Pair up with another student to rehearse and perform one of your solfa melodies for your classmates.

Take the other solfa melody you have created and write it onto the stave below, using crotchets. Look back at the scale of C on page 112 to help you transcribe your solfa melody onto the stave.

Let's sight-sing the three melodies below.

Create a 4-bar sight-reading exercise. Transcribe it on the stave below. Space has been given for you to write your final draft. Together with your classmates, compile these exercises using software like Finale, MuseScore or Score Creator to produce a sight-reading booklet for your class to use.

Final draft

What stuck with you?

Evaluate your learning in this chapter. List what stuck with you and new key words.

Earlier in this book we looked at the importance of **rhythm** in music. Rhythm is an instinctive quality in humans and is within each one of us. Percussion instruments can be traced back to the earliest human communities.

Body percussion is likely to have been one of the first forms of performance – music which is created by the body through actions such as clapping, slapping, stomping and vocalising. Our body has lots of sounds to be explored.

◆ Clicking fingers ◆ Stomping feet

◆ Slapping thighs ◆ Popping cheeks

 Pair up and work together to find four more.

Let's be creative!

Work together to create a distinctive rhythmic pattern using these sounds. Perform them together for your classmates.

Writing body percussion down so others can perform it can be done in different ways. For instance:

◆ Rhythm patterns can be written on a stave or rhythm line.

◆ Words or letters can represent the actions. These could be written below the rhythm patterns on a stave.

L	R
Left	Right

◆ Simple pictures or symbols can be used like icons to illustrate the actions.

Have a go at these examples:

This is written as a rhythm pattern on a single stave line. It uses **hand-claps**, hand-**slaps on knees** (shown by L and R) and **finger-snaps**.

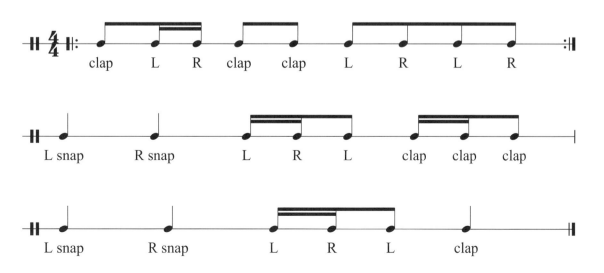

2

This is set out on a five-line stave, with the different lines indicating different sounds. The bottom line, in this case, has foot-stomps, indicated L or R for left or right. If you like performing this body-rhythm, you'll get a chance to incorporate it into a song later in this chapter.

L   R   clap   L   R   clap knees   Shhh

There are eight boxes in the grid below. Illustrate or notate a body percussion pattern below, to fit eight crotchet beats. If you want a beat (or half a beat) of silence, draw a crotchet or quaver rest into the box.

beat 1	2	3	4
5	6	7	8

The possibilities with body percussion are endless, there's so much fun to be had exploring different sounds and patterns. Because it's so physical, it becomes dance and not just sounds.

Think about how to vary the sounds and control them in different ways. For instance, listen carefully to the contrasts within loud and soft clapping or tapping. Here are just some of the things you can try:

Hands	Tapping palm with two fingers
	Clapping cupped hands
	Clapping flat hands
	Rubbing hands together
	Clicking (snapping) fingers
	Flicking fingers
	Tapping fingernails on table or floor
	Slapping knees or thighs
Feet	Tapping
	Stomping
	Sliding left to right
	Tapping toes on floor
	Heel-to-toe tapping
	Clicking heels
Mouth	Shhh sounds
	Popping tongue on roof of mouth
	Popping air-filled cheeks gently
	Popping inside of cheek

Can you add other techniques with their own distinctive sounds?

Rhythm games

Stand in a circle with your classmates, compose and gradually build up a rhythm. One student begins by making one body-percussion sound. The next student repeats this sound but adds their own sound to it – and so on.

Remain in your circle. One student volunteers to perform a rhythm pattern using a body-percussion sound for an 8-beat count. Each person should take a turn at creating a pattern. Try to recall your pattern and write it down on the rhythm line below.

Group performance: 3-part body percussion

Split into three groups. Each group takes one of the lines below. Work together to rehearse your rhythm pattern. When all three groups have their own part fluent and dynamic, come together to perform it.

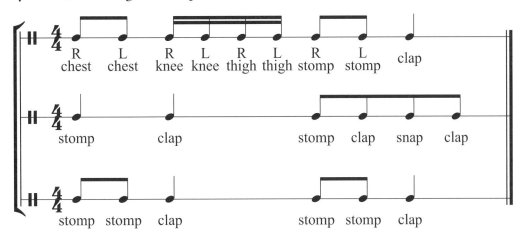

Identify which beats your group wants to emphasise. Experiment, trying different ones. Tempo and dynamics are important too. Work as a team, and you will have great fun performing this pattern. After each rehearsal, evaluate how it sounds and adapt the pattern to work better if needs be.

Once you are confident at performing the group piece, use the lines provided below to create a new three-part body-percussion rhythm pattern to perform in your next class. Go back to the list of sounds above for ideas. Use rests to punctuate the rhythm. Once written, make sure you rehearse together before performing it. Get it sounding really good.

Record your creation using technology software available to you such as GarageBand. Record each track separately, combine and play back to hear the rhythmic patterns in sync.

'Thula Klizeo'

This is a great song for combining singing with body percussion. It was written by Joseph Shabalala, founder of the South African vocal group Ladysmith Black Mambazo (pictured right), while he was in New York. The words express his homesick feelings.

Thula Klizeo (be still my heart)
Nala pase kiya (even here I am at home)

Ladysmith Black Mambazo performing

'Thula Klizeo' performed by Elementary Honor Choir

Piano accompaniment to 'Thula Klizeo'

Joseph Shabalala

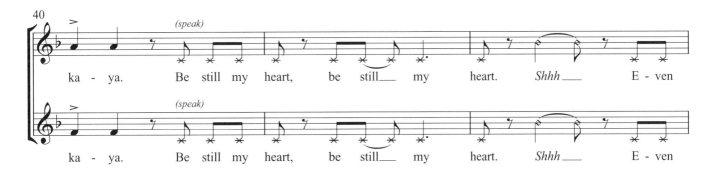

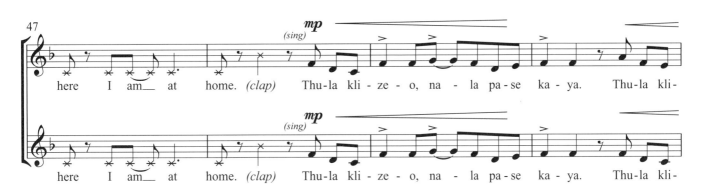

Sight-clapping

Sight-clapping is another form of **sight reading**, concentrating on rhythms. Read the rhythm pattern and clap it out loud. To be confident at reading rhythm patterns, you need good knowledge of the time-values of notes. Sight-clapping helps musicians to hear how the rhythm of a piece of music should sound before they play it on their instrument.

Imagine now this pattern should sound then attempt to clap it.

When you clap long notes, for instance the minims in bars 1 and 2, they still sound short. You should hear the fourth beat in your head, or you could use a percussion instrument that can play a longer sound, like a tambourine.

Can you recognise these songs from clapping the rhythm patterns below?

Here are some more clapping exercises. Take time to study the rhythm before you begin clapping. Try to hear it in your head. You might find a meteronome helpful when clapping these patterns.

Rest	Number of beats
▬	
▬	
𝄽	
𝄾	

? Test yourself

Clapping as a prominent musical feature

Flamenco is a traditional Spanish style of music and dance in which clapping plays an important part. Search online for 'flamenco clapping' and you will find many good examples.

Clapping Music

Search for 'Clapping Music Steve Reich' online to see a performance of *Clapping Music*, written by Steve Reich in 1972. The clapped rhythm is performed as a sort of round:

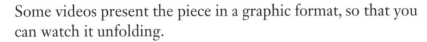

Some videos present the piece in a graphic format, so that you can watch it unfolding.

Singing and Remembering

How is your musical memory? Can you name two songs that you remember completely?

_____

_____

Memory singing is like playing Chinese Whispers. Imagine that someone sings a melody into your ear and asks you to pass it on, singing it into the ear of another person. You have to concentrate on what you hear to pass on the correct melody to the next person.

 Listen to these short melodies and sing them back. For each one, you will hear the tonic note first ('do' in tonic solfa), followed by the tonic chord. Listen carefully, three times, then sing the melody back together.

 This is not easy at first, but with practice your musical memory will develop. Think of all the songs you can recognise, just from listening to the intro! Singing back a melody you've just heard is a great way of training both your voice and your musical memory.

What stuck with you?

Evaluate your learning in this chapter. List what stuck with you and new key words.

Preparing a Song for Performance

Make sure you know the basic facts about the music you want to perform:

◆ Time signature   ◆ Tempo

◆ Key, key signature and range   ◆ The name of the composer and the lyricist

It is also helpful to have an understanding of the background of the piece. Find out as much about the music as possible.

We often receive a printed programme when we go to a **live** performance. What information is usually included? Why do composers and performers choose to share this information with us? Every piece of music has a unique combination of elements which can be appreciated. Sharing information about the composer, the inspiration for their work, the story or mood of the music, the instruments chosen and things we should listen out for can all be identified and explained to us in a programme note.

Choose one of the songs you have performed this year and write a short programme note for it. Good research skills will be required! Include background information, features of the melody, and a musical signpost or point of interest we should listen out for.

Song title	Composer	Genre
Information		
Points of interest		

Performance project

Choose a piece of music you would like to perform. Research and perform it and write about your findings below. Give reasons why you have chosen this music. Discuss the musical features you think listeners might enjoy.

Include a line of the melody on the stave below if you can.

The story of 'Amazing Grace'

Do you know the song 'Amazing Grace'?
Let's sing it together. Here are the lyrics
for verse 1:

> Amazing Grace, how sweet the sound
> That saved a wretch like me!
> I once was lost, but now am found,
> Was blind, but now I see.

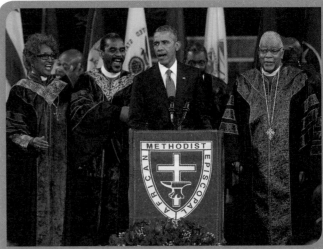

President Obama Singing 'Amazing Grace' at the College of
Charleston during his eulogy for Carolina State Senator Clementa
C. Pinckney and other victims of a mass shooting, 26 June 2015

'Amazing Grace' is a frequently performed **hymn**.
It is called a 'spiritual' and talks of religious
jubilation. Many acclaimed performers have
sung it. Famously, President Obama sang it at
a memorial service to the victims of a gun attack.

So who composed this beautiful melody
and wrote those famous words?

The words were penned by John
Newton, who lived from 1725 to 1807.
He led a turbulent life in his youth,
went to sea and became involved
in the slave trade. After surviving
a violent storm off the coast of
County Donegal, he became a devout
Christian and eventually a clergyman.
He wrote the words to 'Amazing
Grace' around 1772, probably for use
in the church where he was a curate.
Their association with a traditional
tune originally called 'New Britain'
came later, and this gradually evolved
into the version we know today.

Donal Kearney

This mosaic
platform was
created by local
artist Andrew
Garvey-Williams

Newton was commemorated in 2013 when a viewing platform at Lough Swilly,
near Castle Bridge, County Donegal was built. It marks the spot where Newton
supposedly came ashore after the storm of 1748, which was a turning point in his life.

Appraising performances

Being an audience member at any performance is an honour, an opportunity to value
the skills and talents of other members of our school community.

Appraising performances will help to inform your own performance. Discuss with
your class what you feel are the elements of or criteria for a good performance. Invite
a senior student to perform for your class before their practical exams. Ask them to
introduce a piece of music they decide to perform for you.

Performance Appraisal Form

Title of piece _____

Composer _____

Performer _____

For each aspect of the performance, tick the first, second or third column.

	Consistently good	Good, but some mistakes	Could be improved
Musical qualities			
Correct notes			
Good rhythmically			
Good tempo			
Use of dynamics			
Use of articulation			
Control of instrument or voice			
Overall style			
Presentation			

Indicate what you like best about this performance.

_____

_____

_____

Identify what you have learned from this performance that you can apply to your own performances.

_____

_____

_____

What stuck with you?

Evaluate your learning in this chapter. List what stuck with you and new key words.

Reflection and Evaluation Sheet

Unit title:

Music I listened to:

Learning and exploring

I really enjoyed…

Something interesting I learned…

New key words

I excelled at…

Skills I developed in this unit…

My biggest challenge was…

This unit reminded me of learning about…

I overcame this by…

I would like to learn more about…

Goal setting…

-
-
-

Rate your learning

Playing the Recorder

In this unit

Learning to play a musical instrument is a hands on rewarding activity. In this unit you will manage your own learning though practise and discover the benefits of remaining motivated to stick with a new and challenging task – recorder playing. In learning to play the recorder you will improve the quality of your own creations and develop fluency and technical skill as you practise and perform on your own and with your classmates. You will demonstrate your understanding of musical elements, instrumental techniques and develop technical control and fluency in your performances. You will begin to compile a portfolio of pieces for performance.

Intended learning

Perform music at sight through playing, singing or clapping melodic and rhythmic phrases.

Explore where chord changes occur in extracts from a selection of songs.

1.4, 1.7, 1.12 2.4, 2.5, 2.6, 3.5, 3.9

Rehearse and present a song or brief instrumental piece; identify and discuss the performance skills and techniques that were necessary to interpret the music effectively.

Prepare and rehearse a musical work for an ensemble focusing on cooperation and listening for balance and intonation; refine the interpretation by considering elements such as clarity, fluency, musical effect and style.

Design a rhythmic or melodic ostinato and add layers of sound over the pattern as it repeats, varying the texture to create a mood piece to accompany a film clip or sequence of images.

Recorders are versatile instruments. They can be played solo or in groups. They are often accompanied by other instruments such as harpsichord, guitar or piano. Much folk and popular music is suited to recorder performance. In the hands of a skilled player, genres like Irish music, blues and jazz come to life in a special way.

Hold the recorder with your left hand at the top and your right hand at the bottom. Next, get your fingers into position over the holes.

Left hand
First three fingers over the top three holes
Thumb over the hole at the back
Little finger *not used*

Right hand
Four fingers over the remaining four holes
Thumb underneath, supporting the recorder

On most recorders the bottom section swivels, so that your right little finger can comfortably cover its hole (normally a double hole).

To make your first sounds on the descant recorder, blow gently into it, using the first finger of your left hand to cover the top hole and your thumb to cover the hole at the back, and your right thumb just to support the lower half. As you blow, make the sound 'du' into the mouthpiece, starting with your tongue on the roof of your mouth, just at the back of your front teeth, then releasing it. If you cover the two holes cleanly, you will get a nice clear note, the note B. Experiment with covering more holes. As you do so, you will get lower notes.

Covering the holes is harder than it looks. Most of the squeaks recorders make are caused by air escaping through partially covered holes. Use the fleshy part of your fingertips, and keep your fingers close by when not using them. Then you can change notes smoothly when needed.

Sit upright, imagining you have a balloon between your back and the back of your chair, elbows up (not leaning on the desk) and with both feet planted on the floor.

First three notes: B A G

Here are finger charts for those three notes. Can you see how the chart tells you which holes to cover? Make sure you always use the correct fingers and that your left thumb is covering the hole at the back.

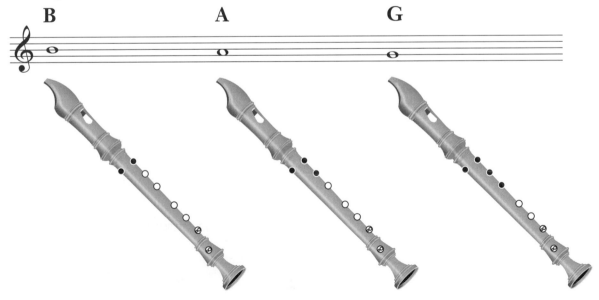

Rehearse these three notes until you are playing nice and cleanly, with no squeaky leaks. Pair up with another student in your class, play around with these three notes, and try to find a melody you recognise using the three notes G, A and B.

Transcribe any melody you have recognised or created together on the staves below.

Try these tunes. They only use those three notes.

All through the night

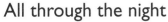

German folk song

All through the night, the moon is sil - ver bright. Cri - cket sings his ti - ny song, sings it through the whole night long, All through the night.

Mary had a little lamb

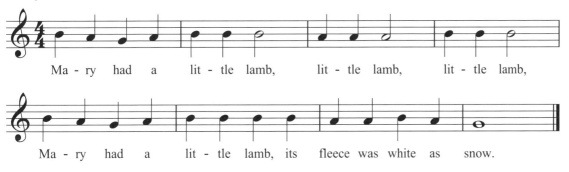

Ma - ry had a lit - tle lamb, lit - tle lamb, lit - tle lamb, Ma - ry had a lit - tle lamb, its fleece was white as snow.

Fais do-do

French lullaby

Hot cross buns

Hot cross buns,   Hot cross buns,   One a pen-ny, two a pen-ny, Hot cross buns.

Suo gân

Welsh song

Win - ter creeps,   Na - ture sleeps;   Birds are gone,   Flowers are none.

Fields are bare,   Bleak the air,   Leaves are shed: All seems dead.

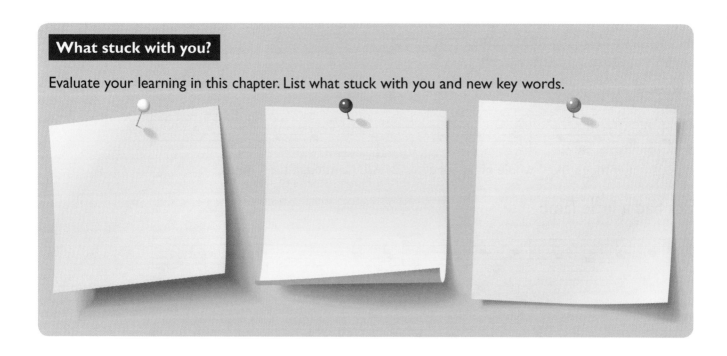

What stuck with you?

Evaluate your learning in this chapter. List what stuck with you and new key words.

Progressing to C and D

New note: C

New note: D

Practise changing between C and D:

And between D and B:

This exercise uses the five notes you have learned so far:

Compose a similar tune and notate it on the staves below.

The marching gospel song 'When the saints go marching in' uses the five notes you have learned. It begins on the note G. Below you will see the words, but only the first four notes written on the stave. Can you and your partner work together to find the rest of the notes and write them onto the stave?

Oh when the saints_____ go march - ing in,_____

_____ oh when the saints go march - ing in

Once you have notated it on the stave, clap it to ensure you have the rhythm correct. Perform it together for your class.

Piano accompaniment to 'Little John'
CD 2 Track 34

Little John

German folk song

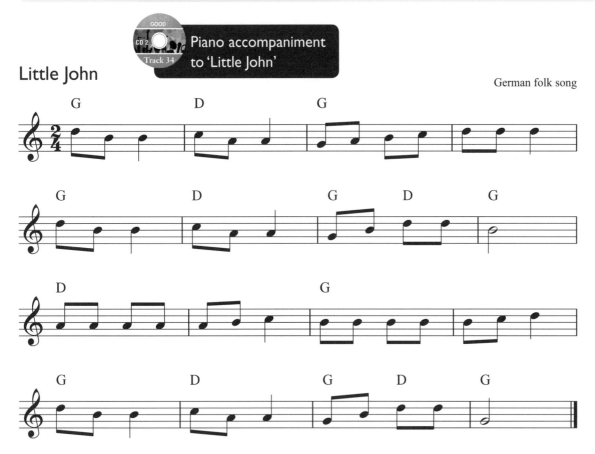

The letters above the stave indicate **chord symbols**. 'G' means a G major chord. You will learn more about chords next year. For now, ask your teacher to show you how to play a simple chord accompaniment on piano or guitar or whatever is available. It will add something to the recorder tune! You can practise on the keyboard diagram on the cover of this book.

Now the day is over

S. Baring-Gould

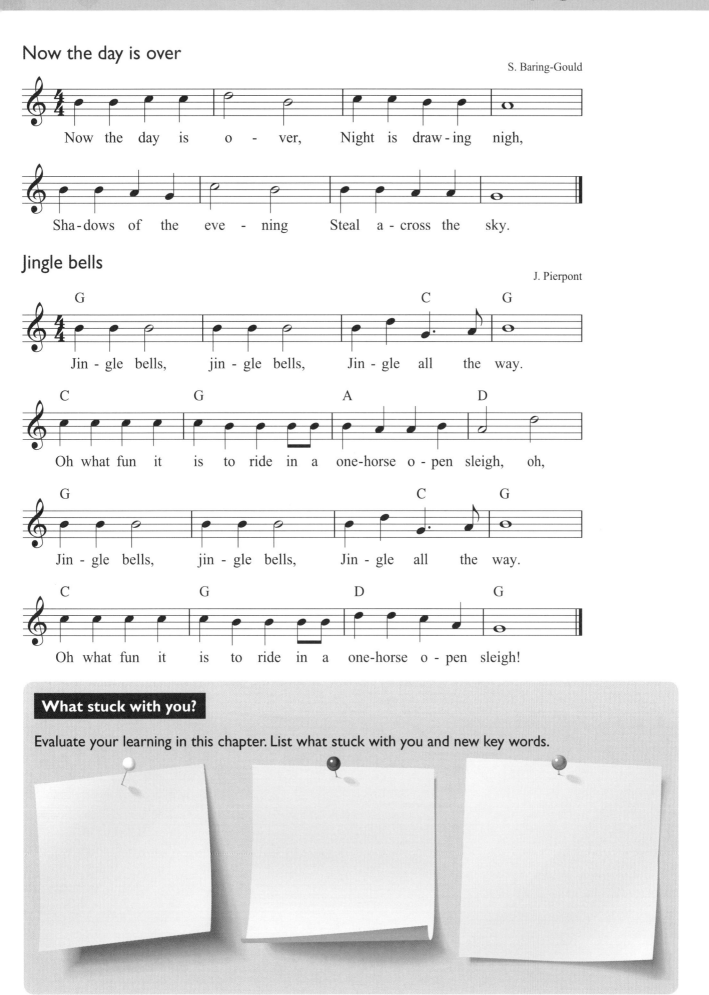

Now the day is o - ver, Night is draw - ing nigh,

Sha - dows of the eve - ning Steal a - cross the sky.

Jingle bells

J. Pierpont

Jin - gle bells, jin - gle bells, Jin - gle all the way.

Oh what fun it is to ride in a one-horse o - pen sleigh, oh,

Jin - gle bells, jin - gle bells, Jin - gle all the way.

Oh what fun it is to ride in a one-horse o - pen sleigh!

What stuck with you?

Evaluate your learning in this chapter. List what stuck with you and new key words.

New note: low D

Managing myself

Make yourself a practice schedule. All new skills take time! Use a practice chart to schedule time to rehearse.

Mon	Tues	Wed	Thurs	Fri	Sat
✓		✓			

London's Burning

Lon-don's burn - ing, Lon-don's burn - ing, Fetch the en - gine, fetch the

en - gine, Fire! fire! fire! fire! Pour on wa - ter, pour on wa - ter.

Try performing 'London's Burning' as a two-part **round**, with the second part two bars behind the first.

Hot Cross Buns

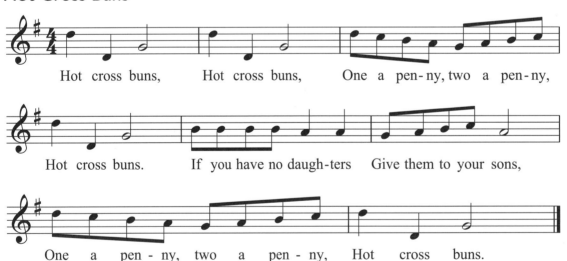

Hot cross buns, Hot cross buns, One a pen-ny, two a pen-ny,

Hot cross buns. If you have no daugh-ters Give them to your sons,

One a pen - ny, two a pen - ny, Hot cross buns.

Scavenge for these features

Find	Where is it? (bar)	Explain feature
Octave leap		
Repeated notes		
Desending melody		

This famous tune was composed by Beethoven for his Symphony No. 9.

Ode to Joy

Beethoven

p

Scavenge for these features

Find	Where is it? (bar)	Explain feature
Tied note		
Leap of a 6th		
Range of song		

Activity

Collaborate with other classmates to create a rhythmic ostinato to accompany this tune, using percussion instruments. Take turns to perform your ostinato along with the music. How does it sound?

Listening

Search online for 'Beethoven Symphony No. 9 last movement' and you will be able to hear what Beethoven did with this melody. At first Beethoven quotes from the earlier movements of the symphony, then the 'Ode to Joy' is presented quietly on strings. Gradually it expands to encompass the full orchestra and then choir and soloists. The way Beethoven brings it to a climax was revolutionary at the time, and still sounds amazing.

New note: low E

Old MacDonald had a farm

Experiment with **found sounds** or instruments to **illustrate** the animals in this song.

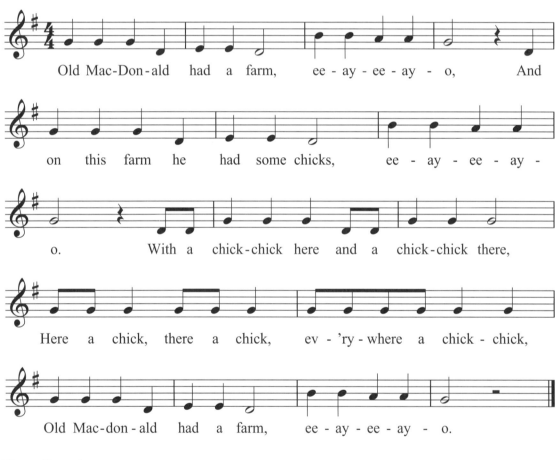

Tom Dooley

Red River Valley

Piano accompaniment to 'Red River Valley'

Chord symbols are shown above the stave. These provide a chordal accompaniment; your teacher can show you how to play the chords. As you listen to the melody, can you sense how the melody-notes, together with the rhythm, suggest where the chord changes should be, and how that leads to a satisfactory **chord progression**?

Skye Boat Song

Speed, bon-ny boat, like a bird on the wing,   On-ward, the sail-ors   cry.

Car-ry the lad   that's born   to be king   O-ver the sea   to   Skye.

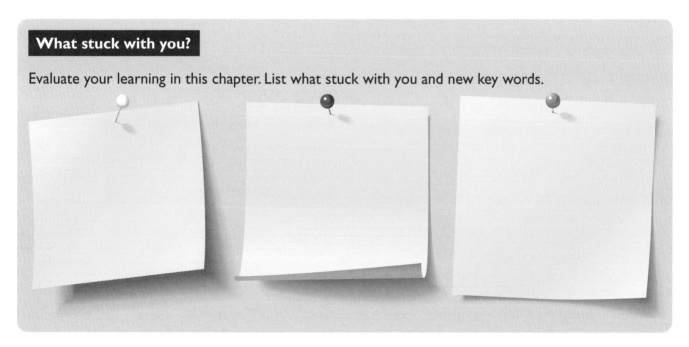

What stuck with you?

Evaluate your learning in this chapter. List what stuck with you and new key words.

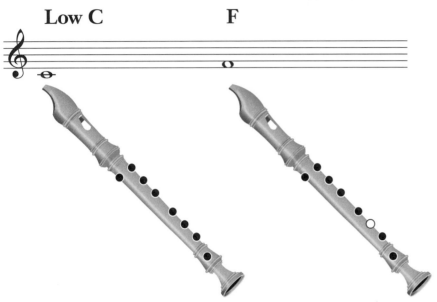

These two notes are more difficult to play, and low C is the most difficult of all, because you have to cover *all* the holes without any leaks. It is the lowest note on the descant recorder's range. Do you know what that means?

Improve your recorder skills

Recorder exercises are a good way to develop your skills. Practise the following exercises to improve your knowledge of these new notes. Clapping the rhythms before playing will help you get them right.

I (C major scale)

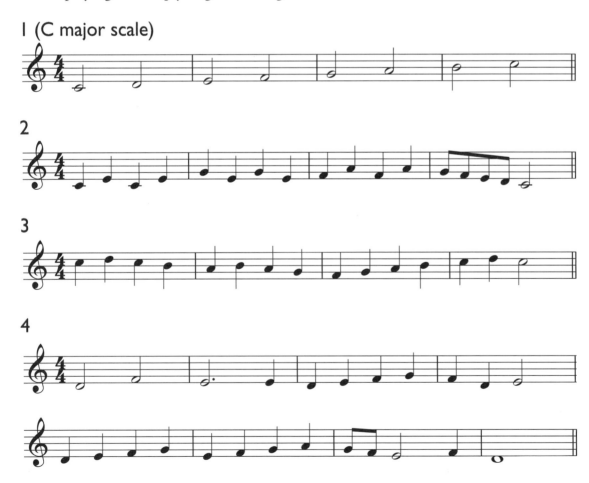

5

Here we go round the mulberry bush

Here we go round the mul-b'ry bush, the mul-b'ry bush, the mul-b'ry bush.

Here we go round the mul-b'ry bush on a cold and fros - ty morn - ing.

Caring for Your Recorder

Recorders can squeak if air is escaping, but this can also be caused by blockages: dust or food particles. Keeping your recorder clean will improve the tone and quality of your playing.

To clean your recorder you will need the following:

◆ Cleaning rod: this should have come with your recorder

◆ A piece of soft cloth: a strip of dish cloth will do

◆ Basin or sink

◆ Warm water

◆ Dishwashing liquid

◆ Dry towel

1 Cover the air hole on the top of the mouthpiece and blow hard two or three times to unclog any obstruction.

2 Dismantle your recorder and wash it in lukewarm water. Rinse and dry.

3 Thread a piece of dishcloth through the eyelet on the top of your cleaning rod and secure it by tying a knot. Reconnect the parts of your recorder and insert the cleaning rod into the bottom of the recorder. Clean the inside of the recorder by twisting the cleaning rod around.

This is an effective way of cleaning the recorder. It will only take a few minutes, but once completed you should hear a clearer tone when you play.

Piano accompaniment to 'Oh Sinner Man'

CD 2 Track 36

Oh Sinner Man

African American spiritual

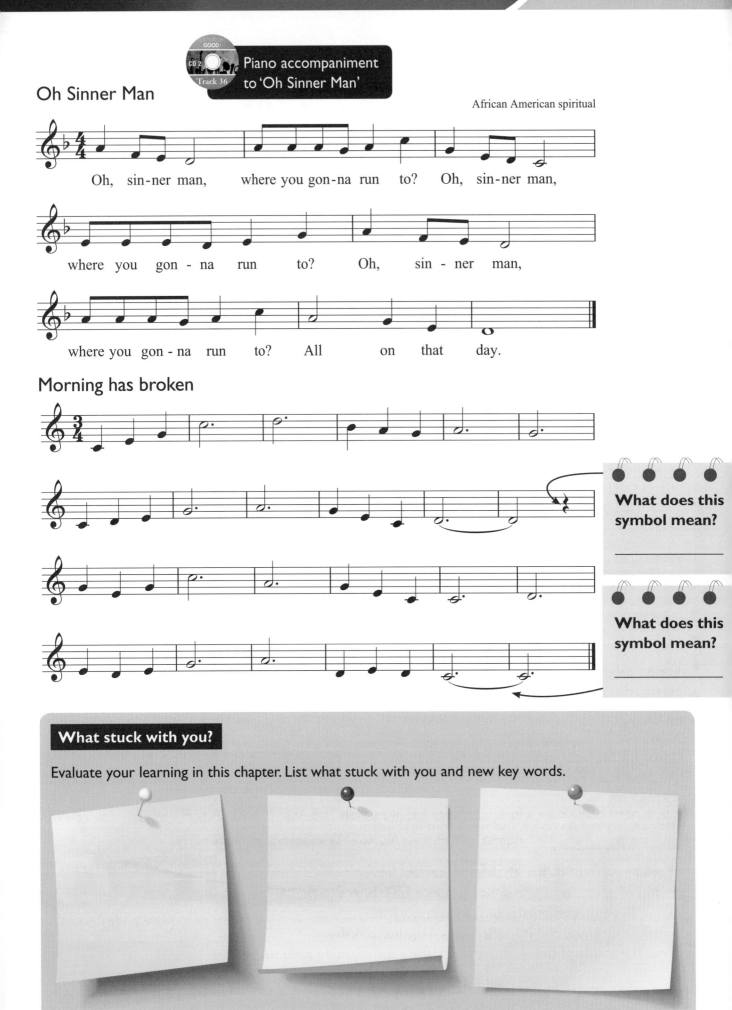

Oh, sin-ner man, where you gon-na run to? Oh, sin-ner man,

where you gon - na run to? Oh, sin - ner man,

where you gon - na run to? All on that day.

Morning has broken

What does this symbol mean?

_____

What does this symbol mean?

_____

What stuck with you?

Evaluate your learning in this chapter. List what stuck with you and new key words.

New note: F sharp

Au clair de la lune

French folk song

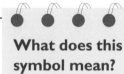

What does this symbol mean?
_____

The Birds' Wedding

This is a duet for two descant recorders.

The tick is a helpful symbol showing you where to breathe.

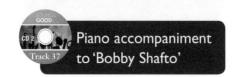

Piano accompaniment to 'Bobby Shafto'

Bobby Shafto

'D.C. al Fine' means go back to the beginning and play until 'Fine'.

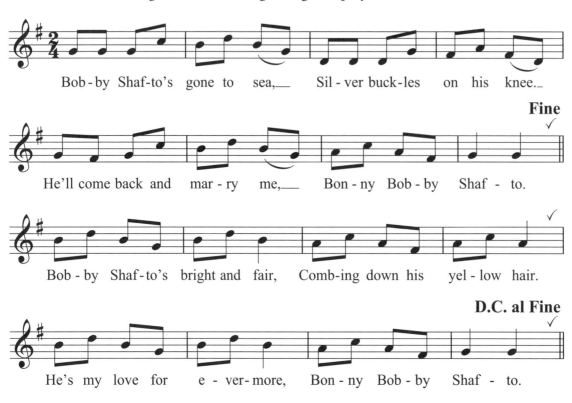

Bob - by Shaf-to's gone to sea,___ Sil - ver buck-les on his knee.___

Fine

He'll come back and mar - ry me,___ Bon - ny Bob - by Shaf - to.

Bob - by Shaf-to's bright and fair, Comb-ing down his yel - low hair.

D.C. al Fine

He's my love for e - ver-more, Bon - ny Bob - by Shaf - to.

The fall and rise of the recorder

The recorder was known as the 'English flute' in earlier times. Composers like Bach and Handel used the recorder for many of their compositions, and recorders have featured in the plays of Shakespeare.

The oldest surviving recorder dates from about 1400 AD. From the fifteenth century, instrument makers began producing families of recorders in a range of sizes, known as **consorts**.

From about 1750, orchestras no longer included the recorder, and it was slowly forgotten. The modern flute replaced it and grew in popularity. In the twentieth century its use revived, and now recorders are among the most widely played of all instruments.

There arc five common sizes of recorders in the recorder family. The smallest is the sopranino and the largest is the bass. There are other sizes, even smaller or even larger, but these aren't often encountered. The most frequently learned are the descant (also called the soprano) or the treble recorder (also called the alto).

From left to right: descant, treble, tenor and bass recorders

New note: high C sharp

> Do you have any recording equipment in your school? Try making a recording of a performance of this song.
>
> You may find that the recording software offers possibilities to add effects to your recording, for instance **reverb** (short for **reverberation**, which is a bit like echo) or **distortion** of some kind. If so, you could experiment, see what effects you get and whether you like them.
>
> The app **GarageBand** will allow you to complete these recording tasks. You can also learn lots more about chords and how they sound. Go explore!

Summer is icumen in

This can be performed as a **round**, with a second part coming in after 2, 4 or 6 bars – or with more than two parts.

Articulation

Articulation marks tell musicians to play notes in a certain way. Good use of articulation can enhance a piece of music, making it sound interesting, lively or flowing. It can help to bring out a melody.

Slurs and staccato dots are two articulation marks commonly used in recorder music.

A **slur** is a curved line joining notes to show that they should be played *legato*, smoothly.

A **staccato** dot placed above or below the notehead means it should be played short and detached.

We will compare different articulations on the next page.

Play this exercise, first **legato** and then staccato. Make both ways of playing effective, but bring out the different character.

The next exercise is good for improving your recorder skills. Play it together.

Now here is the same exercise with articulation added. Learn to play it together. Do you agree that the articulation markings make it more interesting to play and listen to?

Add dynamics to this piece

Why would they enhance this performance?

_____

_____

Play the following 4-bar exercise and work in pairs to decide what articulation would work well. Mark your staccato dots or legato slurs in pencil, in case you change your minds.

Perform your favourite solution to the class.

Lullaby (by Brahms)

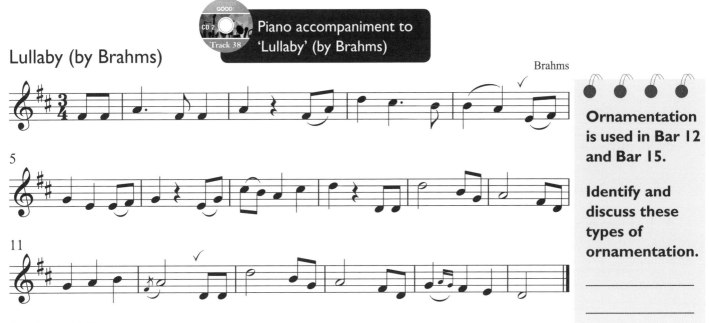

Brahms

> ● ● ● ●
> **Ornamentation is used in Bar 12 and Bar 15.**
>
> **Identify and discuss these types of ornamentation.**
>
> _____
> _____

Barbara Allen

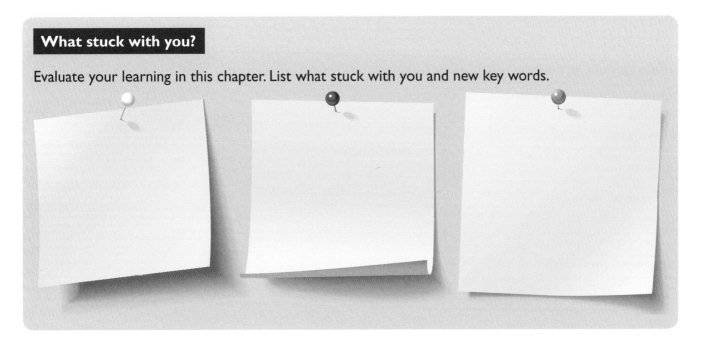

Incidental music

Look back over all the recorder tunes you have learnt. Can you think of any situations in which some of them could be used to accompany and illustrate a theatrical presentation of any sort? The tunes could help tell the story, or they could accompany the action as **incidental music**.

> ### What stuck with you?
>
> Evaluate your learning in this chapter. List what stuck with you and new key words.

Performance Questionnaire

1 What should musicians consider before choosing a piece of music to perform?

_____

2 Identify what performance skills you developed this year.

_____

3 List two pieces of music you have performed this year.

_____

_____

4 Outline what difficulties you faced when preparing for your performance.

_____

_____

5 How did you feel after you performed?

_____

6 List three benefits of performing with others.

_____

_____

_____

7 Do you have any advice for students learning the recorder?

_____

8 Argue why rehearsing music together is important.

_____

_____

9 Indicate what you consider makes a good performance.

_____

_____

Reflection and Evaluation Sheet

Unit title:

Learning

Music I listened to:

Learning and exploring

I really enjoyed…

Something interesting I learned…

New key words

I excelled at…

Skills I developed in this unit…

My biggest challenge was…

This unit reminded me of learning about…

I overcame this by…

I would like to learn more about…

Goal setting…

-
-
-

Rate your learning

Classroom-Based Assessments (CBAs)

There are two Classroom-Based Assessments (CBAs) in Junior Cycle Music. Both are assessed at a common level and relate to specified learning outcomes set out in the Music Specification. CBAs are linked to the learning experiences provided over three years of study and are assessed at the end of year 2 and year 3 of Junior Cycle. Work presented for both CBAs will be monitored and supported by your teacher.

Classroom-Based Assessments	Format	Student preparation	Completed
Composition Portfolio	Two pieces chosen by the student from his/her portfolio	Compositions are produced over time with support and guidance from teacher	Towards the end of Year 2
Programme Note	Individual or group programme note in chosen format	During a maximum of 3 weeks, with support and guidance from teacher	Term 2 of Year 3

CBA1: Composition Portfolio

This is an opportunity for you to compile evidence of your creative accomplishments. The purpose of this assessment is to recognise and celebrate the musical compositions you create over the three years of junior cycle. These projects should reflect your musical ideas and creative expression across a variety of genres. Two pieces from your portfolio of compositions will be selected by you for assessment.

Some suggested creative projects set out in the Music Specification include:

◆ Responding to an auditory or visual stimulus

◆ Arranging an existing piece of music

◆ Creating an answering phrase to an existing phrase

◆ Adding music to a text

◆ Responding to a story or a literary text

◆ Creating an advertisement jingle

◆ Devising a piece of electro-acoustic music

◆ Creating an anthem or a musical piece for a school event

◆ Composing music in response to a personal experience

> **Relevant LOs include:**
> 1.1, 1.2, 1.3, 1.4, 1.12
> 2.1, 2.2, 2.3, 2.7
> 3.4, 3.5, 3.9

Some important information to consider when compiling your portfolio:

◆ You must include any draft work relating to your work

◆ The compositions you work with can be from any recognised musical style or genre

◆ It can be written for instrument or voice and for solo or group

◆ It can be presented in written, digital, visual or audio form, or any other suitable format

◆ A student reflection note must be included with each of the pieces submitted

◆ You may work in pairs or groups but it will be your individual role and contribution to the work that is assessed

A space has been provided for you to compile two samples of work for your Composition Portfolio on pages 197 and 198.

CBA1 Composition Portfolio

Compiling evidence and reflecting on your learning experience.

PORTFOLIO

Date _____ **Name** _____

Topic: _____

Task: _____

_____

_____

Context

Where did you get ideas for this composition and what could this creation be used for?

_____

My Skills

My creation!

Evaluating and Reflecting

What did you learn from this process and what would you do differently next time?

Notes:

_____

_____

_____

_____

CBA1 Composition Portfolio

Topic: _____

Task: _____

_____

_____

Compiling evidence and reflecting on your learning experience.

PORTFOLIO

Date _____ Name _____

Context

Where did you get ideas for this composition and what could this creation be used for?

_____

My Skills

My creation!

Evaluating and Reflecting

What did you learn from this process and what would you do differently next time?

Notes:

_____

_____

_____

_____

Classroom-Based Assessment 2 (CBA2) – Programme Note Guidelines

The Programme Note is intended to illuminate the content of the upcoming performance in an interesting and relevant way. It includes:

◆ a brief introduction to the composers/ songwriters (if applicable)

◆ a description about the historical context of the pieces and the circumstances surrounding the composition

◆ one interesting musical point in each piece for the listener/audience to listen out for

◆ famous exponents of a tune or an instrument

◆ the student's role in a group performance.

The Programme Note can be presented in a written, digital, visual or audio form, or any other format that is deemed suitable. There must be a reference to each of the three pieces in the Programme Note. You will need to include some facts on the composer or the songwriter, some interesting points about the purpose behind the composition and some musical highlights so that the audience or the listener can be alerted to and be aware of the context of the pieces for your practical examination.

Whether you are performing as a soloist or as part of group, or a combination of both, you will still need to provide an individual programme note, but the note on the group performance should include a comment on your role and contribution to the group performance. If you are the composer of any of the pieces that comprise your programme for the practical examination, you should comment on and reflect upon these questions above in the same manner. The challenge is in creating notes that cater for this range and provide something of interest to both the well informed listener and the novice listener.

This Programme Note will need to be completed two weeks in advance of the practical examination and it is advised that you spend no more than three weeks on researching and completing it. You may find it easier to complete your Programme Note as you learn your pieces as this research will also inform your practising and refining of these pieces in preparation for the practical examination.

In considering what information to include you could ask yourself the following questions for each piece:

◆ Who is the composer/songwriter of this piece?

◆ Why did the composer/songwriter write this music?

◆ If the composer or songwriter is unknown (for example in the case of some traditional music or folk music) what type of instrumental or vocal piece is this?

◆ Who are some famous exponents of this type of traditional or folk music?

◆ What was happening in the composer's country at the time of this composition?

◆ Is this piece typical of the time it was written or collected in?

◆ What is the most interesting moment in this piece for me?

◆ What do I want the attention of the listener to be guided towards?

◆ What is or where is my favourite section of this piece?

Relevant LOs include:
1.10, 1.11, 1.13, 1.14
2.4, 2.5, 2.10
3.2, 3.7

The structure of the Programme Note is left to your discretion, and you have the choice and the flexibility to present this in a format of your choosing, and in a way that allows you to focus on the aspects relevant to your upcoming performance. Programme notes are usually accessed by people with a wide variety of background knowledge.

Glossary

Accompaniment	Music which has been composed to support the main part or melody.
Aisling	A patriotic traditional Irish song in which a woman personifies Ireland.
Articulation	Particular ways of playing or singing. Performance techniques which affect the way single notes or groups of notes sound.
Ascending	Music which moves from lower to higher notes.
Ballad	A song which tells a story. Typically each verse has the same melody.
Ballet	A theatrical work with music and dancing.
Barline	A vertical line which separates bars or measures of music on a stave.
Baroque	The musical era from 1600 to 1750.
Baton	Stick held by conductors, used to mark the time signature and guide musical expression in performance.
Beat	The unit of time in a piece of music. The upper number of a time signature indicates the number of beats per bar.
Binary form	A musical form with two sections, A and B.
Body percussion	Sounds made using parts of the body (e.g. foot stamping, thigh slapping).
Bow	Used by string players to pull across the strings of instruments such as a violin, viola, cello or double bass. It is essentially a stick which is strung with hair.
Canon	A form of strict imitation where one part leads and other parts follow with the same or closely related notes, at a distance.
Ceili band	A group of traditional musicians who play music for dancers.
Chance music	A modern style of composing where some elements of the performance are left to chance.
Chord	Two or more notes sounding simultaneously.
Chord progression	A series of chords sounding one after another, also known as a harmonic progression.
Clan song	Traditional Aboriginal song.
Classical era	Generally considered as 1750 to 1830.
Clef	A symbol placed at the beginning of each stave, used to indicate pitches.
Col legno	A performance instruction to use the wooden back of the bow while playing a stringed instrument.
Common time	A time signature notated as a C, indicating four crotchet beats per bar or measure.
Composer	A person who creates and writes music.
Concerto	A piece of music for solo instrument with orchestra.
Conductor	A person who, by means of gestures, leads an ensemble performance, indicating tempo, expression and other aspects of the music.
Consort	Instrumental ensemble, typical of the Renaissance and Baroque eras, e.g. recorder consort.
Copyright	A form of intellectual property, applicable to creative work including art, literature and music.

Countermelody	A melody which is secondary to the main melody. Also known as a countersubject.
Crescendo	Becoming louder. Or a dynamic marking instructing performers to gradually play louder.
Da Capo al Fine	Da Capo (DC) is Italian for 'from the beginning'. This marking instructs performers to return to the beginning of the music and play 'al Fine', which means to the end.
Descending	Music which moves from higher to lower pitches.
Dialogue	Music which is suggestive of a conversation taking place between instruments.
Dictation	Listening and transcribing a rhythm or melody onto a stave.
Diminuendo	Becoming quieter, or a dynamic marking instructing performers to play gradually quieter.
Downbeat	The downward stroke of a conductor's baton to indicate the first beat of the bar.
Duet	A musical ensemble of two singers or instruments, each playing an individual part.
Dynamics	The relative musical loudness or quietness of a performance.
Elements of music	The key components of music: pulse, duration, tempo, pitch, dynamics, timbre, texture, form, expression, tonality.
Ensemble	A group of instrumental performers or singers.
Episodes	A contrasting idea or motif in a composition. e.g. in a rondo, between the repeating sections.
Fanfare	A short ceremonial piece of dramatic music played typically by brass instruments. Often used to announce the beginning of an important event or to welcome an important person.
Film score	Music composed for a film. Its purpose is to illustrate and enhance the story.
Folk music	Traditional songs which originate from a specific country or culture, passed on and preserved in the oral tradition. Many versions of such songs can exist.
Form	Describes the structure/layout of a piece of music.
Found sounds	Sounds created from everyday objects (e.g. pens, paper, water, etc.).
Free rhythm	Music which is not rhythmically organised using a time signature.
Fugue	A short melody or melodic phrase, heard in one part and successively taken up by other parts.
Fusion	The blending of contrasting musical styles or genres.
Gapped scale	A scale used in traditional Irish music which omits certain notes.
Genre	A category or classification of musical style.
Grace notes	A form of ornamentation. Grace notes are printed smaller to indicate that they are subsidiary to the main melody.
Graphic notation	A form of notation using shapes or lines or images instead of conventional music notation.
Harmony	When a combination of simultaneously played notes produce a sound that is pleasing to listen to.

Hertz (Hz)	A unit of frequency, e.g. of vibrations. A frequency of 10 hertz means ten vibrations per second.
Homophonic	A musical texture in which a main melody is supported by block chords.
Hornpipe	Traditional Irish dance tune in 4/4 time with a slow tempo.
Hymn	A religious song composed for congregations to sing together.
Illustrative music	See Programme music.
Interval	The distance from one pitch to another.
Imitation	Instrumental performers or singers repeating a motif or melody in close succession, creating polyphony. Similar to Fugue.
Improvisation	Spontaneous musical creation, often based on an existing melodic or harmonic fragment.
Incidental music	Music composed for use with, for instance, a film, play, television programme, or computer game, as a background or to reflect a narrative, or to enhance a particular atmosphere.
Jig	Traditional Irish dance in 6/8 time.
Jingle	A short advertising slogan, verse or tune which is easily remembered.
Key signature	Sharps and flats indicated at the beginning of each stave to identify the key.
Lament	Song or poem which is an expression of grief or sorrow.
Leap	A jump in a melodic line of an interval greater than a 2nd.
Ledger line	Short lines used to extend the pitch above or below the five lines of the stave.
Legato	Playing notes in a smooth and connected way.
Live music	A live performance in front of an audience, by a single musician or a musical ensemble.
Lullaby	A cradle song or instrumental piece, normally slow tempo and with a soothing, gentle rhythm.
Macaronic	A song which has lyrics in two different languages.
Measures (American)	A bar of music.
Melisma	A form of ornamentation which uses a succession of pitches per syllable, common in sean-nós.
Melody	A sequence of pitches, and the rhythm in which they occur, making a distinct entity.
Metronome	A device used to mark an exact tempo, to help performers to stay in time.
Modal	Music composed using modes that are neither major or minor in tonality.
Modern era	Generally, music composed from 1900 onwards.
Monophonic	A musical texture consisting of one single unaccompanied melodic line.
Mood	A predominant emotion illustrated in a piece of music.
Motif	An important or recurring rhythmic or melodic idea in a piece of music.
Music map	A visual representation of the structure, form or content of a piece of music.
Mute	A device used to muffle or quieten an instrument. Commonly used with brass instruments.

Neumes	A symbol used in music notation during the Middle Ages.
Non-traditional feature	Musical features present in a piece of music which are not typically associated with the style or genre of the music.
Octave	From the Latin for 'eight', an interval of eight diatonic steps between pitches.
Oral tradition	A form of communicating culture and traditions through word of mouth. Passing on historical traditions from one generation to the next without written instruction.
Orchestration	Conceiving and arranging music for an orchestra to perform.
Ornamentation	Adding notes to a melody to decorate the tune. Trills, rolls or grace notes are all examples of ornamentation.
Ostinato	A repeated rhythmic or melodic pattern used in the accompaniment, typically sustained throughout a piece of music.
Patron	Someone (or an organisation) who employs or gives financial support. Composers often worked under patronage.
Pitch	How high or low a sound or note is.
Pitched percussion	Percussion instruments capable of producing distinct pitches, e.g. xylophone, timpani. As opposed to unpitched percussion instruments which produce sounds of indefinite pitch, e.g. cymbal, snare drum.
Pizzicato	A performing technique where string players pluck strings rather than bow them.
Planxty	An Irish harp tune composed in honour of a patron, associated with Turlough O'Carolan.
Playlist	A compiled list of recorded music, chosen for a particular reason or purpose.
Polyphonic	A musical texture where two or more melodic lines are heard simultaneously.
Prepared piano	A modern technique where objects are placed within the piano to alter its sound.
Programme music	Descriptive instrumental music composed to illustrate a picture, tell a story or create a mood.
Programme note	Written information for the benefit of listeners.
Quartet	An ensemble with four singers or instrumental performers.
Range	The distance between the lowest and highest pitches available on an instrument, or used in a piece of music.
Reed	A piece of cane that vibrates in the mouthpiece of a woodwind instrument.
Reel	Traditional dance in 4/4 or 2/4 time. Fast in tempo.
Renaissance era	In music, generally considered to be 1450 to 1600.
Rests	Musical symbols indicating the absence of sound.
Reverb (reverberation)	Also known as 'echo': the prolongation of a sound, acoustically or electronically. Sometimes used to recreate the natural effects of room reverberation.
Rhythm	A strong, regular or repeated pattern of sound.
Romantic era	In music, generally considered to be 1830 to 1900.

Rondo	A musical form where a main melodic idea returns between other episodes, represented as ABACADA.
Round	A musical composition in which two or more voices or instruments perform the same melody with each part beginning at a different point.
Scale	Pitches organised in ascending or descending order. Common scales include major, minor, and chromatic scales.
Score	Printed music which communicates a composition to performers.
Sean-nós	Traditional style of Irish singing.
Sight-reading	Reading and performing a piece of music from sheet music without prior knowledge of it.
Sight-singing	Singing a melody from sheet music without prior knowledge of it.
Slow air	Traditional Irish tune played in free rhythm. The melody is often derived from a sean-nós song.
Sonata	Multi-movement instrumental work.
Sound source	Any object which can vibrate to produce a sound.
Soundwave	The vibrations in the air that carry sound from a sound source.
Spiral score	Experimental graphic format of notating music.
Staccato	Short, detached notes. A form of articulation represented by a dot above or below the notehead.
Step movement	When a melody moves from one note to an adjacent note, without leaping.
Syllable	The part of a word that contains a single vowel sound, pronounced as one unit. 'Flute' has one syllable, 'trumpet' has two syllables.
Symphony	A substantial work, often multi-movement, written for orchestra.
Tempo	The speed or pace of a piece of music.
Ternary form	A musical form in which the first section returns after a middle section, represented by the letters ABA.
Texture	Describes the density or layers present in a piece of music.
Theme	A musical motif or idea which is interwoven through a work, can form the basis of an entire composition.
Timbre	The unique tone, colour or quality of any sound or instrument.
Time signature	A pair of numbers, one above the other, showing how many beats there are in each bar, and what note value represents each beat.
Tonic solfa	A system of naming pitches in a scale using syllables rather than letters.
Traditional feature	The musical elements that typically distinguish an established style or genre.
Trio	A composition for three performers or in three parts.
Unison	When all singers or instrumentalists perform the same melody together.
Upbeat	The beat before the first (strong, accented) beat of the bar.
Variation	Changing a main theme or melody, developing it rhythmically, melodically or harmonically.